- How many times have you done something foolish when you thought you'd never do anything like that again?
- Do "little white lies" often get away from you because you can't quite handle the truth?
- What do you do with that juicy bit of gossip you just heard?

Solomon knew all about our tendencies to act impulsively, irrationally or emotionally, and in his Proverbs, he has an answer for many of the circumstances we encounter. His common sense approach speaks to everyday situations.

Proverbs for Easier Living

Special Crusade Edition printed for
the Billy Graham Evangelistic Association

world wide
publications

1303 Hennepin Avenue
Minneapolis, Minnesota 55403

Jo Berry

Other good Regal reading:
Can You Love Yourself?
   by Jo Berry
Up to Heaven and Down to Earth
   by Fay Angus
Yet Will I Trust Him
   by Peg Rankin

This special edition is published
with permission of the original publisher.

The foreign language publishing of all Regal books is under the direction of GLINT.
GLINT provides financial and technical help for the adaptation, translation and
publishing of books in more than 85 languages for millions of people worldwide.

For more information write: GLINT, P.O. Box 6688, Ventura, California 93006.

Published by Regal Books
A Division of G/L Publications
Ventura, California 93006
Printed in U.S.A.

Library of Congress Catalog Card No. 80-50540
ISBN 0-8307-0748-4

Dedication

*To Brenda, Cathy and Brian
for making my life so full and
being the blessings they are.*

Contents

Introduction

At times each of us bemoans the fact that life isn't easy. Periodically we are plagued with problems, face failures, make wrong decisions and suffer tragedy and loss. We all have our frustrations, joys, heartaches, happiness, successes, and failures, but when the bottom line is written, frequently it is our approach to our circumstances, and not the situation, that makes life easy or difficult.

On the surface it may look as if some people have all the luck while others are destined to an overdose of bad breaks; but closer analysis reveals that luck isn't something people "have," it is something they create. Yes, life is sometimes unfair, hurtful and discouraging, and, depending on the way you choose to live it, it will be a worthy experience or an endurance test. Many times, in our human imperfection, we make life harder than it actually is or needs to be.

The common sense standards by which we should live our lives are recorded in the Bible, and those standards that tell us how to live peacefully and fruitfully with ourselves and our fellowman are centered in the book of Proverbs. It literally overflows with principles and practicalities that, when applied, can make our lives easier.

What I have tried to do in this book is define some biblical guidelines for easier living, show what results we can expect if we use them, and make practical suggestions about how to implement their usage in everyday situations. I know from my own experience and from watching and talking to friends and people I meet that these ground rules can make life more pleasant, less complicated and easier to live.

ONE

Wising Up

The beginning of wisdom is: Acquire wisdom.
Proverbs 4:7

Have you ever done something then, almost as soon as you did it, wonder how you could have acted so foolishly? Have you ever had a disagreement with someone then gotten into a full-blown argument because you lost control of your temper and said things that were unwarranted or you didn't mean? Or have you intensified problems between yourself and your husband by goading or nagging him and making snide remarks? Maybe you've told a lie to get out of trouble then gotten in deeper because you didn't tell the truth.

I'm afraid all of us create difficulties for ourselves because we act impulsively, irrationally or emotionally. We do not behave wisely. We act on impulse rather than sensibility. If we want easier lives we need to "wise up."

Contrary to popular belief, wisdom is not some mystic,

ethereal quality we get when we are old and gray. According to *Webster's New World Dictionary,* it is the power of judging rightly; following the soundest course of action, based on our experience, knowledge and understanding. It is using common sense.

Proverbs rightfully has been called, "The Book of Wisdom." It is crammed with witty, humorous, profound truths that can help us develop that precious commodity and, therefore, live less stressful, more satisfying lives. For example, Proverbs observes that you will avoid unnecessary quarrels and friction if you stay calm and collected without raising your voice or doing verbal battle since "a gentle answer turns away wrath, but a harsh word stirs up anger" (Prov. 15:1).

Proverbs illustrates the futility of nagging, noting that "the contentions of a wife are a constant dripping" (19:13), that "it is better to live in a desert land, than with a contentious and vexing woman" (21:19) or "better to live in the corner of a roof, than in a house shared with a contentious woman" (21:9). Proverbs emphasizes the danger of lying, warning that "a false witness will not go unpunished, and he who tells lies will perish" (19:9).

Because of its common sense approach to everyday situations, Proverbs is probably the most practical book in the Bible. Billy Graham said that the book teaches us how to get along with our fellowman. I would take that a step further and say it also teaches us how to live with ourselves. It speaks to all the contemporary issues facing us today: religion, sex, drugs, money, the work ethic, greed, hatred, fear and anger. It mirrors our foibles to us and instructs us, in detail, how to live wisely and well.

Proverbs is also a book about life-styles. If we are going to acquire wisdom, which is the foundation for easier living, we need to incorporate into our lives the godly behavior patterns presented in Proverbs. At first they may seem odd, old-fashioned and restrictive. We have been so brainwashed by the world for so long that what is normal in God's sight may seem abnormal to us; but if we believe and use the Proverbs we will be happier and more fulfilled.

Wising Up About Sex

A large portion of the first 10 chapters of Proverbs is devoted to sexual attitudes. We are living in a time when sex dominates every facet of our lives: advertisers use sex to sell everything from toothpaste to tires; promiscuity is rampant; living together has become as acceptable as getting married; thousands of children are born out of wedlock each year; abortion is thought by many to be a valid means of birth control.

This kind of preoccupation with sex is nothing new. It was just as prominent in Solomon's time when Proverbs was written; so the book is laced with warnings about sexual excess. We are admonished to stay away from any adulterous person who has forsaken his or her marriage vows; to avoid "the strange woman, . . . the adulteress who flatters with her words; that leaves the companion of her youth, and forgets the covenant of her God" (2:16,17).

The first 14 verses of chapter 5 caution us to steer clear of improper sexual behavior. They plainly state that illicit sex—sex outside of the bounds of marriage—is a sin. This is true for men or women, for those who are single or married regardless of their age, race or religion.

Conversely, Solomon extols sex within the marriage relationship. He sets forth, through the power of the Holy Spirit, a beautiful case for monogamy and marital sex, emphasizing that fidelity makes for a joyful, exhilarating relationship. "Rejoice in the wife of your youth. As a loving hind and a graceful doe, let her breasts satisfy you at all times; be exhilarated always with her love" (5:18,19).

It is clear that sex within the proper context is not dirty. God invented it. "Male and female He created them. . . .

And God saw all that He had made, and behold, it was very good" (Gen. 1:27,31). The Lord instituted the one-flesh relationship. He meant for sex within marriage to be a pleasurable, fulfilling experience; a God-given gift to enhance the love relationship between man and wife.

Sex is not dirty, but misuse of it tarnishes and defiles it. Sex outside of marriage, either premarital, extramarital or homosexual, is sin. it is misuse of that great gift.

The Proverbs depict, in vivid detail, the seduction process and the temptations that we face in this area. The tempter will "flatter with words" (see Prov. 2:16) and have a "smooth tongue" (6:24). His or her lips "drip honey," and his or her speech is "smoother than oil" (5:3). The person who stirs a sexual response will be physically appealing and will try to intrigue his or her victim in subtle ways, so we are warned, "Do not desire her beauty in your heart, nor let her catch you with her eyelids" (6:25).

The Proverbs also repeatedly warn about the dire consequences of improper sexual behavior, and there are many. Proverbs 5:10 illustrates the waste that accompanies illicit sex. It says, "Strangers [will] be filled with your strength, and your hard-earned goods [will] go to the house of an alien." The success and possessions we attain in marriage are lost on a lover. Loyalty, as well as money, property and family are disregarded in an erotic sexual relationship.

Proverbs 5:11 apprises us of the dangers of venereal disease. "You groan at your latter end, when your flesh and your body are consumed." Even today, not all venereal disease is treatable. A new strain, which severely affects the unborn fetus, which does not respond to any standard medical procedures, has surfaced. Frequently in women, by the time symptoms of syphilis or gonorrhea appear, it is too late to prevent sterility and in some cases death. That is why the apostle Paul observed that sexual license is a sin against your own body (see 1 Cor. 6:18).

Proverbs 5:12-14 show the depression, guilt, embarrassment and loss of respect that accompany indiscriminate sex. "And you say, 'How I have hated instruction! And my heart spurned reproof! And I have not listened to the voice of my teachers, nor inclined my ear to my instructors! I was almost in utter ruin in the midst of the assembly and congregation.' "

Proverbs 6:33 says a person who commits adultery will find "wounds and disgrace . . . and his reproach will not be blotted out." That's quite a price to pay for fleeting pleasure and momentary passion.

An anonymous proverb muses, "If you play with fire you'll get burned." This is certainly true of sexual indiscretion. "Can a man take fire in his bosom, and his clothes not be burned? Or can a man walk on hot coals, and his feet not be scorched? So is the one who goes in to his neighbor's [mate]; whoever touches her [him] will not go unpunished" (6:27-29). And once again the pages of God's Word stress the severe ramifications for adultery or fornication.

In his handbook, *Wise Living in a Foolish Age,* Jim Cecy points out that, while "it is often said that sex sins affect few people but those directly involved, this is far from the truth."[1] He uses the example of an unmarried man and woman who engage in intercourse, and says, "That one sin affects the man himself, the woman herself, the man's parents, the woman's parents, the man's and woman's immediate families (brothers, sisters, etc.), the man's future mate, the woman's future mate, their future in-laws, their friends and their church families," especially if it comes to a place where public discipline is needed.

So a wise life-style means we will appreciate the God-created gift of sex and adhere to the Lord's regulations on how to use it. We must be committed to the concept that *all* sex outside marriage is sin and that abuse of it extracts a heavy personal toll, both physically and emotionally.

Wising Up About Drugs

The world is consumed not only with sex, it is also hooked on drugs. Any mind- or emotion-altering chemical that can bring a "high" or blot out reality, or relieve fear and anxiety is classified as a drug. In the era in which the Proverbs were written, there was not the abundance of drugs we have today. Certain plants and ointments were known to create a euphoria or ease pain, but the drug that plagued society then is one that is still with us—alcohol.

Alcohol *is* a drug. It is addictive. And the degeneration which excessive drinking causes in a person is similar to the damage that overuse of any drug will cause: it destroys body, soul and spirit. Therefore, I think we can apply God's standards for use of alcohol to any of our present day stimulants or depressants. I am not going to discuss the moral pros and cons of drinking but examine what the Proverbs say about misuse of alcohol or any other drug.

Proverbs 20:1 says, "Wine is a mocker, strong drink a brawler, and whoever is intoxicated by it is not wise." So right off we see that *getting drunk is not smart*. Why? Because wine is a mocker. It holds us in contempt, lets us do and say things that open us to derision and ridicule. It depresses our inhibitions and encourages us to make fools of ourselves.

Why else is drunkenness foolish? Because *strong drink is a brawler*. It lowers our resistance and lets tempers flare. Barroom fights are an institution. Many murders, especially in families, are committed by someone who has been drinking.

Overuse of drugs affects performance. We use the word "spacey" to describe someone who is tripping out on pills. We say a person is "out of it" when he is high or drunk. Proverbs 21:17 observes that, "He who loves wine . . . will not become rich." Alcohol dulls the senses and slows reactions. Someone under its influence does not think clearly or perform well. Many people who use drugs excessively lose their jobs, as well as their incentive. The person who "loves" wine will not be successful at anything but being a drunkard.

In the twenty-third chapter of Proverbs, Solomon penned a word portrait of a drunk, showing what happens when alcohol is misused. He began by illustrating the state of mind and the attitude of a drunk. "Who has woe? Who has sorrow? Who has contentions? Who has complaining? Who has wounds without cause? Who has redness of eyes? Those who linger long over wine, those who go to taste mixed wine" (vv. 29,30).

Drug abusers have *sorrow, contentions and complaints because they cannot control their lives*. They are at the mercy of the drug they use and of the people around them, many of whom take advantage of their unstable condition. They have wounds without cause because drunks cannot control their bodily functions. They fall, stumble and bump into things. Statistics show that over half of the drivers involved in automobile accidents have been drinking or are under the influence of drugs. And red eyes are the trademark of those who overindulge.

Sin often comes in pretty packages and that is certainly true of alcohol, which entices and induces us to partake. "It sparkles in the cup . . . it goes down smoothly"; therefore, it is best not to "look on the wine when it is red" (see v. 31). Examine a magazine ad for wine or hard liquor. It usually portrays a beautiful couple looking into a sunset or sitting before a glowing fire or having dinner by candlelight, toasting each other with warm affection.

Most restaurants in California serve liquor. When our family was having dinner out the other night we started talking about how "yummy" the drinks that were being served to the various tables looked. Rich creamy chocolate browns, pretty pinks, with slices of orange and pineapple decorating the glasses; bright red cherries on top; big fat olives, mounds of whipped cream. They are structured to appeal to the senses.

Other drugs—pain killers, sleeping pills, tranquillizers and such—entice by the relief they promise. Pop a pill and erase a care. They appeal to the emotions.

Solomon quickly brings us face to face with reality and the penalty paid for drunkenness. He reminds us that these enticing potions "at the last bite like a serpent and sting like a viper" (see 23:32). They inflict sudden pain, poison the body and cause sickness, headaches and sometimes death. And if you drink too much for too long, you get what is commonly known as the DTs, when "your eyes will see strange things, and your mind will utter perverse things" (23:33).

A person who has freaked out on drugs loses control of his faculties. He is "like one who lies down in the middle of the sea, or like one who lies down on the top of a mast" (23:34)—staggering, falling down, experiencing dizziness and vertigo.

In the final stages, and this is true of many drugs, the user loses his memory. He blanks out, and cannot remember what happened to him, where he has been or what he did. He says, "They struck me, but I did not become ill; they beat me, but I did not know it" (23:35). Anyone who is at the mercy of drugs has no control over what happens to him. He is a slave to his habit and it controls what he does, where he goes and who his associates are.

The ultimate penalty for misuse of drugs is addiction. In spite of the pain, the humiliation, the expense and the physical suffering, all an addict wants is more of whatever drug he is dependent on. The drunk in Proverbs 23:35 asked, "When shall I awake?" Not because he wanted to return to normalcy or recover from his drinking bout but so he could, "seek another drink."

As believers we are supposed to be controlled by God, to be filled with His Spirit, so if we let anything enslave us we are not living wisely. We must maintain a life-style of reliance on the Lord, not on artificial, impermanent, debilitating crutches, such as drugs or liquor.

Wising Up About Money

Just as there is nothing wrong with sex when it is used properly, there is nothing wrong with money or material possessions. Actually, God in His sovereignty decides who gets what. "The rich and the poor have a common bond, the Lord is the maker of them all" (22:2). In some instances financial prosperity is a reward for righteous behavior. "The reward of humility and the fear of the Lord are riches, honor and life" (v. 4).

Money and possessions are not problems; our attitude toward them is. When we get "things" too often we lose our sense of value. We start thinking how great we are to have acquired what we have. We take pride in our belongings and focus onto transitory, temporal possessions, forgetting that God is the source of all we have.

Eventually, if they become too important to us, we depend on material goods for happiness. That is the height of foolishness because, as an old proverb muses, "Money cannot buy happiness." If we are going to "wise up" about money we need to take a look at what riches *cannot* do for us.

For one thing, they cannot buy us favor nor status with God, nor affect His eternal judgments. "Riches do not profit in the day of wrath" (11:4). Neither do they lend stability to our lives because, "He who trusts in riches will fall" (11:28).

Although possessions and money may contribute to our enjoyment, they must never be relied on as the source of it. On the contrary, sometimes wealth brings stress and problems. People think, "If only I had such and such, *then* I would be happy," but when they get what they think they need, the happiness doesn't come so they get even more despondent and depressed.

Dorothea S. Kopplin observes that, "The true values of life are not those that can be measured in dollars."[2] The Proverbs stress that, "Better is a little with the fear of the Lord, than great treasure and turmoil with it" (15:16).

Relying on riches is dangerous because riches are not forever. History has recorded what happened to many wealthy people who lost their fortunes in the stock market crash of 1929. They committed suicide or went insane. When they lost their money, their mansions and their important titles, they lost their identities. They thought they had it made, that their finances meant they were safe and secure. Much to their dismay they learned that wealth is transitory, here today, gone tomorrow.

How can we keep from being trapped by our money and possessions? Perhaps you think personally you don't have enough to cause you problems, but no matter how much or how little any of us has, it is our attitude toward it that matters. Things are only things, no matter how much they cost. They are inert, non-living substances, good only for the pleasure, comfort and assistance they bring to people. If what we have, or what we want but cannot get, makes us unhappy and keeps us from enjoying life, we are letting our possessions control us, as surely as the addict lets liquor or drugs dominate him.

If we are going to live wisely and well we need to develop a perspective about money. One thing is certain. It does not deserve as much attention as we give it. Solomon counseled, "Do not weary yourself to gain riches, cease from your consideration of it. When you set your eyes on it, it is gone" (23:4,5). Rather than relying on mammon, we are to "set [our minds] on the things above, not on the things that are on earth" (Col. 3:2). God alone is eternal so we should concentrate our affection on Him—on that which has lasting value.

Agur, one of the Spirit-inspired authors of a portion of Proverbs, made this request about a proper perspective con-

cerning money and possessions: "Give me neither poverty
nor riches; feed me with the food that is my portion, lest I be
full and deny Thee and say, 'Who is the Lord?' Or lest I be in
want and steal, and profane the name of my God" (30:8,9).

His petition was a wise one. He did not want too much or
too little; just enough to keep him from sinning because of
what he did or did not have. If each of us took that attitude,
how much easier life would be!

Most important, we need to remember that "it is the
blessing of the Lord that makes rich, and he adds no sorrow
to it" (10:22). Blessing, a state of well-being where we rest in
God's grace, is true, lasting wealth. That is what we should
seek after and desire.

A Look at a Wise Woman

In order to help us visualize and internalize the overall
scope of a wise life-style, the Lord included in the book of
Proverbs a beautiful description of a woman who lived in a
manner that was pleasing to Him in every way. She is a
prototype whose actions, attitude and mind-set can serve as
an example of understanding, initiative and common sense
for us all.

When we are introduced to her the first thing we are told
is that she is a loving wife who is totally committed to her
marriage and her husband's welfare. "An excellent wife,
who can find? For her worth is far above jewels. The heart of
her husband trusts in her, and he will have no lack of gain.
She does him good and not evil all the days of her life"
(31:10-12).

She is called excellent, virtuous, so we see that she is
morally good. She is trustworthy. Her husband trusts her
with his *heart!* He is confident that he can trust her with his
life, convinced that whatever she does will enhance their
lives.

We find that she is a cheerful doer and diligent worker.

She is also frugal and thrifty. "She looks for wool and flax, and works with her hands in delight. She is like merchant ships; she brings her food from afar" (vv. 13,14). I have always been encouraged by the fact that she delights in working with her hands, indicating that even menial tasks are pleasurable if approached with the right attitude.

She is portrayed as being unselfish. This wise, loving woman has a servant's heart and even fixes breakfast for her servants. "She rises . . . while it is still night, and gives food to her household, and portions to her maidens" (v. 15). She is also energetic; a hard worker who is committed to whatever task is at hand. "She girds herself with strength, and makes her arms strong" (v. 17).

Not only does she rise early and labor throughout the day, she stays up late, adding hours to her schedule so she can accomplish what must be done. "Her lamp does not go out at night. She stretches out her hands to the distaff, and her hands grasp the spindle" (vv. 18,19). I believe she spends some of those extra hours making the goods she sells in the marketplace. "She makes linen garments and sells them, and supplies belts to the tradesmen" (v. 24).

She is enterprising and industrious. Tailoring and stitchery are not her only means of personal income. She also deals in real estate. "She considers a field and buys it; from her earnings she plants a vineyard" (v. 16). Although we aren't told specifically why she works outside her home, we can assume whatever she gets she uses to contribute to her family's well-being because, "She looks well to the ways of her household, and does not eat the bread of idleness" (v. 27). She also gives of herself and her substance to those who are less fortunate. "She extends her hand to the poor; and she stretches out her hands to the needy" (v. 20).

We can also assume that this *ishshah chagil*, this "woman of force," who has such a far-reaching, positive effect on the lives of so many, never neglects those closest to her. She is in complete control of the sphere God assigned her. She tends to the present while preparing for the future. "She is not afraid of the snow for her household, for *all* of her household [and that includes servants and hired hands] are clothed with scarlet" (v. 21). Even though she lives in a temperate climate she is prepared for the occasional winter storm.

This wise, compassionate woman is truly "other centered." She concentrates on serving rather than being served, on giving rather than getting. As a result, she is happy and satisfied. "She senses that her gain is good" (v. 18). She possesses an equanimity of spirit and peace of mind that come from doing what is morally right. She has no fear of old age. Because she lives righteously, "she smiles at the future" (v. 25), a confirmation that godliness and joy are inseparable.

Although she is unselfish, she realizes it is wise to devote some time to herself and her personal needs. She is not vain but cares about how she presents herself. She puts her best foot forward. She is well groomed. "She makes coverings for herself; her clothing is fine linen and purple" (v. 22).

Her actions and words enhance her physical beauty. "Strength [of character] and dignity are her clothing. . . . She opens her mouth *in wisdom,* and the teaching of kindness is on her tongue" (vv. 25,26). She is a well-mannered, dignified, gracious lady.

What does this virtuous woman reap as a result of wise living? She and her husband both receive acclaim from the community because of her sterling reputation. This fortunate man who, partly because of his wife "is known in the gates, when he sits among the elders of the land" (v. 23), knows how lucky he is. "He praises her, saying: 'Many daughters have done nobly, but you excel them all' " (vv. 28,29).

Her children also pay her tribute. They openly display their admiration and affection. "[They] rise up and bless her" (v. 28). She receives all of this praise, recognition and love because she is a woman who fears the Lord. He is the source of her wisdom: "The fear of the Lord is the beginning of wisdom" (9:10). Her life is a challenging example of what wise living brings.

Wisdom *is* attainable. As we have seen, it centers on God. Wising up requires effort and activity on our part. "Let your heart hold fast my words; keep my commandments and live; acquire wisdom! Acquire understanding! Do not forget, nor turn away from the words of my mouth. Do not forsake her, and she will guard you; love her, and she will watch over you" (4:4-6).

The basic requirement for easier living is wisdom and "the Lord gives wisdom; from His mouth come knowledge and understanding. He stores up sound wisdom for the upright" (2:6,7). "The beginning of wisdom is: Acquire wisdom!" (4:7).

Workshop

1. To help you discover how wise you are according to God's standards, look up each proverb and read it, then rate yourself on a scale of 1 to 10, 10 being the best and 1 being the lowest.

a. Proverbs 17:27:
   I use common sense in both complex   ☐
   and mundane situations.

b. Proverbs 7:4:
   I use knowledge properly.   ☐

c. Proverbs 9:9:
   I recognize when I am doing something   ☐
   foolish or destructive.

d. Proverbs 4:14,15:
   I look before I leap. ☐

e. Proverbs 8:33:
   I ask God for wisdom daily. ☐

f. Proverbs 21:30:
   I compare whatever I think is wise to ☐
   God's standards for wisdom.

g. Proverbs 10:14:
   I am not wise myself so must rely on ☐
   the direction of others who are.

h. Proverbs 5:6:
   My life is quite stable and ☐
   uncomplicated.

i. Proverbs 15:28:
   I know how to ponder and I think before ☐
   I act or speak.

j. Proverbs 24:3,4:
   I feel I usually have control of my life. ☐

k. Proverbs 22:5:
   I am cautious in my approach to people ☐
   and situations.

l. Proverbs 11:3:
   I do what I believe is morally right. ☐

m. Proverbs 15:13:
   I have a sense of humor. ☐

n. Proverbs 8:17:
   I seek wisdom.   ☐

2. Some famous proverbs about wisdom and life-styles
   are listed here. Read each one then write in your own
   words what it means to you.

a. It is a great folly not to part with your own faults, which
   is possible, but to try instead to escape from other people's, which is impossible (Marcus Aurelius).

b. Knowledge comes but wisdom lingers (Alfred Ten-
   nyson).

c. Knowledge is proud that he has learned so much, wisdom is humble that he knows no more (William
   Cowper).

d. To know that which before us lies in daily life is the
   prime wisdom (Milton).

e. Wisdom is ofttimes nearer when we stoop than when we
   soar (Wordsworth).

f. When a man has not a good reason for doing a thing, he
   has one reason for letting it alone (Sir Walter Scott).

g. Don't put the cart before the horse (anon.).

h. Learning without thought is useless; thought without learning is dangerous (Confucius).

i. It is costly wisdom that is bought by experience (Roger Ascham).

j. Everyone hears only what he understands (Goethe).

k. Pleasure admitted in undue degree enslaves the will nor leaves the judgment free (W. Cowper).

l. Pleasure is seldom where it is sought (Samuel Johnson).

m. Money is a good servant but a dangerous master (Bouhours).

n. A fool and his money are soon parted (anon.).

o. Before borrowing money from a friend, decide which you need more (anon.).

Notes

1. Jim Cecy, "Wise Living in a Foolish Age," unpublished paper.
2. Dorothea S. Kopplin, *Something to Live By* (New York: Doubleday and Co., 1945), p 108.

TWO

The Low Cost of Good Living

*In the way of righteousness is life,
and in its pathway there is no death.*
Proverbs 12:28

When I was in the midwest this summer, I watched a local talk show. The host was interviewing the resident of a small town who was celebrating his one-hundred-fifth birthday. The interviewer asked him the inevitable question: "To what do you attribute your long life?"

The old man smiled, leaned forward in his chair and without blinking an eye said, "I did what the good Lord said I was supposed to, didn't do nothin' He said I wasn't supposed to, and never overdid nothin.' "

That man had learned the secret of the low cost of good living, but we live in a world that is populated by people who have not. People are plagued with stress, are unhappy with their jobs, their families and their station in life. Suicide and divorce rates are soaring. Stress is now a major mental health problem. Modern man's technological advances and material accomplishments have not brought him peace and satisfaction, but they have increased his frustration and sense of failure.

Why has this happened? I believe the main reason is because we have lost our direction, our sense of perspective, and have forgotten that happiness comes from living what the book of Proverbs calls a "righteous" life.

Maintaining a righteous life-style does not mean you must be a pious saint who dwells on some supernatural plane or lives in a monastery. It does mean that if you are wise you admit there are moral absolutes and that you can, to a great extent, determine your destiny and the outcome of your circumstances if you act according to certain universal, God-ordained principles.

The world and its philosophers would have us believe that there are no such absolutes. And as they live their "do as you please" and "if it feels good, do it" ethic, their unhappiness and disrupted lives are proof that they are wrong. A sovereign God established a behavior code for all of His creatures to follow, and when they do not they are adversely affected. They pay a price such as poor health, loneliness, depression, lack of love, and a multitude of various social and spiritual problems.

Conversely, living a righteous life—doing what is good, honest, fair and acceptable to God—brings what the Bible calls blessing. I define blessing as "soul joy." It is a peace and pleasantness, an inner sense of well-being, a tranquillity that abides in your human spirit and cannot be negated by problems or external adversity. It is God's reward to those who live righteously. So, if we are going to be consistently happy we need to find out what is involved in living a God-pleasing life-style.

There are two principles in Proverbs that are basic to righteous living which, if we learn and apply them, will guarantee a more joyous, quality existence. The first is that we must *fear the Lord;* the second is that we must *trust Him*.

Fear of the Lord

Proverbs 9:10 says, "The fear of the Lord is the beginning of wisdom." So, if we want to be wise enough to properly interpret God's practicalities for good living, first we need to fear Him.

What is fear of the Lord? When I was a child I thought it meant I was to be afraid of Him, which made it very difficult for me to relate to Him, because it is hard to get close to someone who frightens you. "Fear" was an awesome sounding word that conjured up images of hell fire and brimstone.

Fortunately, that isn't what the word "fear" means. It means to respect, revere and worship. A wise person holds God in high esteem and worships Him in both attitude and action.

Solomon recorded that, "The fear of the Lord is to hate evil" (Prov. 8:13). God is holy; separate and set apart from all that is sinful and evil. He hates sin. Therefore, if we fear Him, we incorporate His value system into our lives and hate everything that is wicked, immoral or iniquitous.

Generally, we fail to do this. We shrug our shoulders at evil, relabel it or ignore it but we do not detest it. Hate is a strong term; it is a consuming emotion. When you hate something, you are repelled by it, hostile toward it and hold it in contempt. You loathe and despise it. Those of us who claim we truly worship and adore the Lord will hate evil and find it intolerable, offensive and unbearable.

For example, my oldest daughter has never liked peas. Even when she was a baby, if I'd feed her a bite of peas she would contort her face, spit them out and shake her head violently. She says there is something about the taste and texture of that vegetable that is totally repulsive to her to the point where just the thought of peas almost makes her physically ill. She hates peas. She is never tempted to eat them.

Likewise, we will not be tempted to behave unrighteously if we hate unrighteousness. If we are as strongly opposed to evil as God is, we will leave it alone. It will be totally repulsive to us.

I have found that my own personal awareness of and revulsion for evil increases if I ask God to help me see it through His eyes; to look at situations from His perfect perspective. In the light of His purity, details I would overlook are magnified and put into focus.

Why should we fear the Lord? Simply stated, because He deserves to be worshiped. Look at the things we venerate in our everyday lives. I know a man who takes better care of his Mercedes than he does his children. He spends hours petting, pampering and polishing it. What about the celebrities we put on pedestals, many of whom flaunt their ungodliness for all to see? Some people worship their pets, others their homes or their jobs. The list of mankind's false gods is endless.

None of these things is worthy of honor. All of them are flawed, imperfect and transitory. But we are told that the Lord was established from everlasting, "From the beginning, from the earliest times of the earth, when there were no depths . . . when there were no springs abounding with water. Before the mountains were settled, before the hills," God was (Prov. 8:23-25). *He* is eternal. *He* is perfect. *He* is worthy of our adoration.

In Psalm 96 the psalmist declared that the whole creation should worship God: all the earth, the nations, peoples, families of the peoples, the heavens, sea, trees, the field and all that is in it. "For the Lord is great, and greatly to be praised: he is to be feared above all gods" (Ps. 96:4, *KJV*).

God is great, magnificent and awesome but because man does not want to attain to His divine stature, he has tried to bring the Lord down to a human level. In the movie "Oh

God!" man reduced Him to a comical, puny, cigar-puffing figure, dressed in tennis shoes, who runs around making mistakes. No wonder people don't fear the Lord. If misconceptions such as these are their only resources, who can blame them?

A wise person gets to know God as He really is, as He is revealed on the pages of His Word. The righteous esteem Him with every breath they take, every word they speak, everything they do. They fear Him.

The Principle of Trust

The second principle that is embodied in righteous living is the principle of trust. "Trust in the Lord with all your heart, and do not lean on your own understanding. In all your ways acknowledge Him, and He will make your paths straight" (Prov. 3:5,6).

There are only two objects of trust: God or self. One is positive, one is negative. One is productive, the other is debilitating. God is faithful, man is not.

We should trust the Lord because we are not trustworthy and God is. He is perfect and we are imperfect. Have you ever failed yourself? I have, many times. How many New Year's resolutions do you keep? How many times have you promised yourself you would stay on your diet, or finish a project, or change in some way, yet failed to carry through? Unlike us, God is completely reliable.

Another reason we should operate on the principle of trust is because life is so complex. Humanly speaking, it is impossible to know always what we should do or when and how we should do it. We need supernatural guidance and instruction to survive as whole, healthy individuals in this topsy-turvy world.

Wisdom would be unnecessary if life were lived in black and white and consisted of a simple system of dos and don'ts, yeses and nos, with no grey or technicolor areas. Then we would face only rudimentary choices of right and wrong.

But life isn't like that. Life is complex and obedience is not as simple as doing one thing or its exact opposite. God's rules and principles may be clear-cut but acting them out is not. Without His guidance we would be lost in a maze of indecision and confusion.

Most of us are not aware of how many hundreds, perhaps thousands, of choices we must make every day. Decisions made in a moment can affect a lifetime. There are numerous demands made on us. One person says, "Do this." Another says, "Do that." We are bombarded with you should, you must, you ought. Everybody wants a piece of our lives, wants us to set our priorities so as to make life easier for them.

Without God's superintendence, our lives would be so complicated and we would be going in so many different directions that we could not function. He has one perfect thing He wants each of us doing at any given time, and if we are trusting Him, He can reveal His will to us. Placing confidence in the Lord simplifies life and makes it immensely easier. "He who trusts in his own heart is a fool, but he who walks wisely, will be delivered" (Prov. 28:26) from confusing complexities.

A final reason we need to trust God is because we cannot see into the future. We must plan and make provisions for it because we live in time and are limited and controlled by it. Yet, what is going to happen is hidden from us. We are warned, "Do not boast about tomorrow, for you do not know what a day may bring forth" (Prov. 27:1). How true that always is!

Just today I had planned to take the entire morning to run errands. But my daughter's car broke down so she is driving mine and I am sitting at my typewriter. Without praying and trusting the Lord as we make decisions about an unknown future, we could not have any peace of mind.

The Plus of Trust

The principle of trust contains both dos and don'ts, shoulds and should nots.

The first "do" is the command to, "Trust in the Lord with all your heart" (Prov. 3:5). The word trust, as it is used here, is a wrestling term. I don't know much about that sport. The only time I watched it was during the Olympics. The thing I noticed was how the challenger would pounce on his opponent, grab hold of and get wrapped up in each other. They stuck to one another like tape sticks to paper.

That is what trust is: clinging to the Lord no matter what happens; adhering to Him and never letting go. In the Hebrew the word *trust* translates "body slam," which is a wrestling term. A body slam is not a casual bumping into someone, or merely being next to him. It involves making an impact, as when two cars collide at high speed. Trust is more than saying, "I believe." It is literally body-slamming onto God and cleaving to Him with all our strength.

Another thing we see in this principle is that the Lord is to be the object of our trust. The Hebrew term used here for Lord is YAHWEH, which is God's covenant name. By using that title He is affirming that He is a faithful God, One who can keep our trust. He is vowing to keep His promises if we will but trust Him to do so.

Then, our trust must be total and complete. In this same verse (3:5) we encounter that little but mighty word, *all.* "Trust in the Lord with *all* your heart." God did not say we are to trust with part of, most of or even 99 percent of our heart but with all of it. Trust is a spiritual absolute! Scripture never tells us to trust God partially or somewhat. We either do or we don't.

Because trust is an absolute, a drop of doubt can negate it. For example, I can't trust my husband only 50 percent of the time. If I don't trust him completely I don't trust him at all. If I believe only part of what my friend tells me, I do not have faith in his or her honesty. You either trust someone or you don't. The same is true with God. It is all or nothing.

The part of our being with which we are to trust is our heart. That word is used frequently in the Bible and refers to much more than a physical organ. It is often interchanged with the word soul, and takes its root from a word that means "to breathe." So, the heart is the part of man which gives him life—that propels him and supplies him with his get-up-and-go.

The concept of the heart embodies five facets of our humanity: (1) our *emotions —the feeling part of our heart; (2) the choosing part of our being which we refer to as our will;* (3) our *conscience,* the component that helps us determine right from wrong, good from evil; (4) *awareness,*the part of our soul that capacitates us to relate to people and things around us, that tunes us in to reality; and (5) the *mind*—the thinking, intellectual part of our human spirit.

Obviously, trusting God with all our heart means we commit our feelings, our volition, morality, consciousness and our intelligence to Him. We cannot withhold in any area or we are not trusting.

Another "do" in the principle of trust is found in verse 6: "In all your ways acknowledge Him." This is practicing the presence of Christ; dwelling on Him, keeping Him in the foreground of your consciousness and constantly giving Him preeminence in your life.

For example, I am married to George Berry. Because he is my husband and I love him, I consider his feelings and his likes and dislikes when I make plans and decisions. I want to please him and do things I know will make him happy. I want to enrich his life and contribute to our relationship in meaningful ways. Wherever I go, whatever I do, I never forget for a moment that I am his wife. Consciously or not, I always acknowledge the fact that I am Mrs. George Berry and submit myself to the reality of our relationship.

Acknowledging God in all our ways means much the same thing. Wherever we are, whatever we do, we bow to the Lord's ultimate supremacy; we never forget for a moment that we are His. We strive to contribute to the relationship and try to please Him. Acknowledgment is submission, in the purest sense.

The principle of trust also incorporates a "do not," something we should not do. *"Do not lean on your own understanding"* (Prov. 3:5). Obviously, we are prone to do just that or we would not be warned against letting it happen. The words *lean on* literally mean "to bend toward." So we are cautioned not to give in to our natural tendency to bend toward our own ideas and solutions.

At the time the book of Proverbs was written, soldiers who stood guard carried spears. Because they had to stand at attention for long periods of time, their weapons were structured to act as a support for them, to be a sort of leaning post, to keep them from swaying or weaving from side to side. In the spiritual sense, we are to stand firm in the Lord rather than wavering from His uprightness and bending our own way.

Leaning on our own understanding implies a falling or drooping when we should stand upright. It is the opposite of body-slamming onto God. This doesn't mean we are not supposed to use our minds but, when we have a choice between doing things our way—which may appear easy, logical, simple and most expedient, or doing them God's way—which may make no sense to us at all, we are to *trust* rather than operate on our human instincts and desires. We are to stand upright toward sinful solutions.

What happens when we trust in this way? "[The Lord] will make your paths straight" (Prov. 3:6). Once we are depending on God, He is already in the process of directing our lives. His direction is not bossiness but guidance with which He smooths the road so we can travel without obstacles blocking or hindering us.

Many of you have probably traveled by automobile on winding, mountain roads. Maneuvering such a course is more treacherous and not nearly as easy or safe as taking a straight, four-lane highway. When we choose our path, we choose the precarious road of our humanity; it will be full of gullies, pitfalls, boulders and detours.

When George and I were engaged, we drove out to California from Kansas during the Christmas holidays so I could meet his family before we got married. We were driving straight through (a 32-hour drive at best) and when we got into Flagstaff, Arizona, we discovered on the map what looked like a much shorter route to Los Angeles, one that cut off over 100 miles. So we took highway 89-A.

We did not know that it wound way up into the mountains. We were not aware that the roads would be icy and that it would be snowing. It took us nine tense, frightening hours to travel those few miles on our "shortcut." We could have reached the same point in two hours if we had taken the main highway. The path we chose looked simple and easy, but it wasn't. We should have consulted someone who knew before we plunged ahead.

Many times, we do in a spiritual sense what George and I did on that trip. We follow our own path rather than God's straight way and end up wasting time, effort and getting involved in some pretty hectic experiences. The shortest distance to any goal in your life is God's straight path.

The Low Cost of Good Living

What is the benefit of walking God's way, of fearing and trusting Him rather than living life on our own terms? The reward we will receive can be summed up in one word: security! "He who listens to [God] shall live securely, and shall be at ease from the dread of evil. . . . He who walks in integrity walks securely" (Prov. 1:33; 10:9).

Security has many aspects. It involves being loved and

accepted, and the Lord has testified that, "I love those who love me" (Prov. 8:17), assuring us that we will receive His affection and concern. Security embodies peace of mind: freedom from fear and danger and agitating passions. Those who live according to God's righteous standards do not have to worry about what will happen to them because of wrongs they have done. An unrighteous person doesn't have that kind of protection. He is constantly faced with reaping the results of his evil deeds, dreading the time when his sin will find him out.

Living a righteous life shelters us from danger or harm. "[The Lord] is a shield to those who walk in integrity, guarding the paths of justice, and He preserves the way of his godly ones" (Prov. 2:7,8). A shield was used by warriors to fend off the weapons of the enemy and to protect their vital, life-sustaining organs. Righteousness is a safeguard, a protective shield.

I recently read an article about a little boy who was born without any physical immunity to germs. In order to survive he has to live inside a plastic bubble, in a completely sterile atmosphere where no germs or contamination can touch him. The air he breathes is filtered and people who touch him do so from the outside, wearing special gloves that are sewn into the side of his impenetrable home. He is sealed off from any external elements that could infect or hurt him in any way.

When we are walking in integrity (acting in accordance with what we know and believe to be right, moral and honorable) we are guarded from the dangerous, sometimes fatal, effects of sin. Evil cannot harm us by invading our existence.

Fear, another by-product of insecurity, is also negated by living according to God's standards. As you walk with the Lord in a trust relationship, "You will walk . . . securely, and your foot will not stumble. When you lie down, you will not be afraid. When you lie down, your sleep will be sweet"

(Prov. 3:23,24). In the United States, in 1979, doctors issued over 33 million prescriptions for sleeping pills. It has been estimated that over one-quarter of the country's population suffers from insomnia; but God promises "sweet sleep" to those who rest in Him. "The fear of the Lord leads to life, *so that one may sleep satisfied,* untouched by evil" (Prov. 19:23, italics added).

The fact that God protects us when we are sleeping is proof of His keeping power. When are we most vulnerable? Obviously, when we are in an unconscious state of some kind. Even when we are asleep, totally unprotected and openly vulnerable, the Lord promises we have nothing to fear. That's security!

Righteous living also assures security because it keeps us from trouble. If we do the right thing, we will not get into trouble for doing what we should not. "The righteous is delivered from trouble. . . . The righteous will escape from trouble" (Prov. 11:8; 12:13). So even when we have problems and difficulties, we will be delivered from them when we are maintaining a proper, godly life-style.

A final security factor in the low cost of good living is that it guarantees us freedom from want. "The Lord will not allow the righteous to hunger" (Prov. 10:3) in either the physical or spiritual sense. He will supply our needs; He knows what they are. We may not get all our "wants" but we will not go without the necessities that make for a healthy body and a prosperous soul.

If someone walked up to you on the street and said, "I promise to supply you with abundant happiness and a good life if you will just trust me, believe in me and do as I say," how would you respond? God has done just that. He has promised that if we trust Him, worship and obey Him, He will give us lives that are overflowing with His blessing. "In the way of righteousness is life, and in its pathways there is no death" (Prov. 12:28).

Workshop

Look up the proverb and list the benefit(s) of righteousness listed in each one. (The first one is an example.)

Reference	Benefits
11:3	*guided by integrity*
11:5	
11:18	
11:28	
11:31	
13:25	
14:14	
15:29	
16:7	
18:10	
19:25	
20:7	
21:21	
22:4	

THREE

Reaping What You Sow

*The deeds of a man's hands
will return to him.
Proverbs 12:14*

Two summers ago, as I was browsing through the garden department of a local discount store, I noticed a sale table piled high with flower bulbs. They weren't wrapped or labeled, which is why they were being sold so cheaply. There was no way to tell what kind of bulbs they were, but since I can never resist a bargain I bought a sackful of them and planted them in a planter that runs the length of our house.

As spring approached I could hardly wait for the bulbs to sprout. True, I didn't know what would bloom but there was one thing I was sure of—I had planted, therefore I knew something would grow.

After Christmas tiny green shoots started poking through the earth. I watched them with great curiosity as they shot upward. When buds appeared I tried to guess what kind of flowers they might be. By May the planter was alive with color: irises, crocuses, daffodils, tulips and an assortment of lilies were blooming in fine array. After months of waiting and expectation I was rewarded with a gorgeous crop, and each year when the bulbs burst forth under my kitchen window I am blessed by the beautiful sight and smells. I continue to reap from what I sowed.

Sowing and reaping is a universal law of nature. Every farmer expects a crop when he plants; he knows that, barring unforeseen or natural disasters, his labor will be followed by a harvest. This law not only applies to the physical world, but God has created within His universe a spiritual ecology, a principle of recompense that governs our behavior.

The Principle of Recompense

Scripture teaches that for everything we do there is a consequence that is commensurate with the deed. This law of recompense, as stated in Proverbs 12:14, says that, "The deeds of a man's hands will return to him." The apostle Paul, in Galatians 6:7, explains it this way: "Whatever a man sows, this he will also reap." In science this dictum is called Newton's Third Law of Motion: "To every force and action there is an equal and opposite reaction."

For some reason, many people approach this axiom from a negative point of view. They see it as a sort of, "If you aren't careful, you're going to get it," warning. And, depending on how they live their lives, that may be true.

I prefer to look at it as a positive, directing force that can make our lives easier and bring us greater happiness and fulfillment because God's Word promises that "he who sows righteousness gets a *true* reward" (Prov. 11:18, italics added). Think of the potential! To a large extent we can determine the results of our actions by what we do and how we do it. Since we can choose what to sow, we can dictate what returns to us.

An old proverb translates it as, "What goes around, comes around." Exactly how does this "carousel theory" work? For example, if you choose to lose your temper you will get turmoil in return because, "A hot-tempered man stirs up strife" (Prov. 15:18). But, if you stay calm and are a peacemaker, rather than an agitator, your life will be more harmonious because, "The [one who is] slow to anger pacifies contention. . . . A gentle answer turns away wrath" (Prov. 15:18,1). We can interpret these kinds of injunctions to mean that what we do boomerangs—it comes back to us in kind.

Usually at this point the resident cynics arise and inform me that I don't know what I'm talking about. They bombard me with their "good guys finish last" philosophy. What they forget is that we cannot expect every punishment that results from unrighteousness to be visible. We do not always know what is going on inside a person's soul—what their inner turmoils, sorrows and frustrations are. All of us would like to see God strike the bad guys with lightning (as long as we don't happen to be one of them), but He does not operate that way. Sin traps the sinner even though the penalties are not always seen.

These same pessimists cite many instances when the good they did was overlooked, rejected; or they bemoan the times they were persecuted for doing what they thought was right. How can anyone argue with that? All of us have had things like that happen to us. Life does seem to operate that way and our own wisdom tells us that if we are going to survive or get ahead we should do unto others before they do unto us.

But do these circumstantial evidences mean that we do not reap what we sow? I think not. I believe it means we don't recognize our reward when it is given to us. We are oblivious to the grace and goodness God bestows upon us.

Too often we miss God's blessings because they come

packaged differently than we thought they would. And we also expect our crop to be something tangible and obvious. Peace of mind, self-respect and a clear conscience are not as readily defined as material possessions or social status.

Last week the newspaper carried the story of a high school student who had written a paper in one of his classes about the importance of honesty. In it he stated that if he ever found a large sum of money he would return it to the owner. He had an immediate test of his belief when he and a companion found over $3,000 in cash. They returned it to the person who had lost it. He gave each of the boys a $50 reward. When the boy was interviewed, the reporter asked him if he was sorry he didn't keep the whole amount. The boy replied, "Absolutely not. Knowing I did what was right is reward enough." He had received his blessing: a peaceful soul.

The main reason we do not recognize our reward is because we are looking to the wrong source for payment. We want plaudits from men and monetary or material compensation. God has promised that "he who sows righteousness gets a *true* reward" (Prov. 11:18). So rather than relying on human sources for what is due to us, we should look to the Lord. Because God alone is just, righteous and perfect love, He is the only being who can legitimately issue that *true* reward. He is the One who blesses us.

That in itself is a benefit because it frees us from seeking the approval of men and from needing to be noticed or trying to gain attention because of the things we do. It also means that as long as our motives and behavior are acceptable to God, we do not have to justify or explain ourselves to others. We will reap what we sow: God will give us our true reward.

Let's take a positive, detailed look at the principle of recompense and see how we can use it in our lives to bear fruit and achieve fulfillment.

The spirit of the law is that we reap whatever we sow.

This law is illustrated in nature—when I planted flower bulbs, flowers grew. If a corn seed is planted, corn grows. Radish seeds produce radishes and rose bushes procreate roses: like begets like. The nature of the crop is determined by what is planted.

Righteousness is imbedded with its own reward, as is sinful behavior. The results that are produced by our actions will resemble those actions. Every deed is followed by its corresponding effect. We reap *whatever* we sow.

The tenth chapter of Proverbs is rich with examples of how sowing and reaping are connected. Proverbs 10:4 says that diligence is followed by riches whereas negligence results in poverty. Proverbs 10:7 promises, "The memory of the righteous is blessed, but the name of the wicked will rot." Verse 10:12 teaches that if we sow love, our other transgressions will be less noticeable but if we sow hatred we will stir up a big crop of strife. And Proverbs 10:16 declares that, "The wages of the righteous is life, the income of the wicked, punishment." In life, as in nature, like begets like.

The problem with too many of us is that we plant the wrong things. Living unrighteously is as foolish as planting weeds. Enough of them grow without any help from us. We don't need to contribute by purposely adding to the crop. Likewise, all of us unthinkingly and carelessly err, so we consistently reap the results of our sin.

We can redirect and better our lives only if we consciously plan to sow enough righteousness to choke out the weeds of our humanity. We need to develop godly life-styles, not leave our fate to chance and hope for the best, because in the end, we will reap *whatever* we sow.

Another basic quality in the law of recompense is that you have to sow before you reap. A seed alone is impotent. In the junk drawer in my kitchen I have packages of tomato seeds, radish and carrot seeds, green bean and cantaloupe seeds, watermelon and onion seeds. (Guess who had good intentions about planting a garden last spring!) They have been there for several months. None of them is growing and none will unless I plant the seeds in the right kind of soil and at the right time of year.

Humanly speaking, good intentions and pleasant thoughts do not matter. They are irrelevant unless they are followed by action. Thinking about visiting a convalescent home or telling your child you love her or planning to drop a note to a friend thanking her for being there with you anytime you need her, or thinking about telling your husband how much you appreciate him is not the same as doing those things. Peter Marshall wisely observed that "small deeds done are better than great deeds planned." The only way you can reap is to sow.

Another core component of this principle of compensation is that once you sow, you will reap. Planting carries with it the expectation of harvest. I remember the first year my son Brian and I planted a vegetable garden. He was four years old. We carefully treated the soil and put the seeds at the recommended depth, placing them perfectly in their holes. Then we covered them with dirt and watered them. When we were finished I told Brian, "Now, all we have to do is wait for them to grow."

Early next morning he was outside, looking at the ground. When I asked him what he was doing he said he was waiting for the plants to start growing. So I had to explain to him that they do not grow overnight but that in a few weeks sprouts would appear. Nevertheless, everyday he checked the garden. He knew the time would come when we would reap what we had sown. He anticipated a return for his labor.

The human counterpart of this law of nature is that once we have done something we can never undo it. The results are beyond our control once a deed has been performed. I could not decide to defy the law of gravity and jump out of a 40-story building then, halfway down, change my mind and go back up. If I decided to break that law I would fall and die. The result is predetermined by my action and, once begun, is irreversible.

The same is true with the law of recompense. Right now the headlines are blaring the tale of a politician who, in a hasty and violent outburst of uncontrolled anger, shot and killed two people. What that young husband and father did is irrevocable; no matter how desperately he would like to erase his crime, he cannot. Once he pulled that trigger it was too late.

A deed, once done, cannot be undone. All we can do is live with the consequences, be they bitter or sweet. The secret, then, is to assure good results by carefully choosing what we plant by controlling the way we live and behave; because there is always a harvest once a crop is planted.

Intrinsic to the concept of recompense is the fact that although we will always reap when we sow, we will reap in season. The apostle Paul said, "In due time we shall reap" (Gal.6:9). "In due time" may be right away or a long time off, because what we do can have one of two results: immediate or remote. Sometimes sowing and reaping embraces both.

I am reminded of Job. He was God's servant, "A blameless and upright man, fearing God and turning away from evil" (Job 1:8). He went through trouble, awesome testing and trials and suffered both physically and emotionally, but eventually, "The Lord blessed the latter days of Job more than his beginning . . . And Job died, an old man and full of days" (Job 42:12,17). The fact that he lived righteously did not save him from problems or grief but ultimately, in due season, what he did came back to him in its own time.

This principle implies that we must consider the final, long term results of our actions rather than immediate satisfactions. What we do now may affect the total scope of our lives and the lives of others, months or even years from now.

This aspect is especially meaningful to me as an author. I wrote my first story when I was eight years old. As I was growing up I wanted to be many things: an airline stewardess (they didn't call them attendants in those days), a teacher, a private detective, a criminal lawyer, but more than anything else I wanted to be a writer. When I was in junior high and high school, I took as many English and journalism classes as I could. I worked on the school paper and kept a very dramatic, if less than accurate, diary each year. And I wrote multitudes of stories and poems.

In college I majored in English. I took classes where I would have to write compositions. Later, when I was teaching elementary school, I enrolled in a correspondence course with a writing school. I wrote curriculum. And I kept writing stories and poems.

It wasn't until I was past 40 that I stopped collecting rejection slips regularly and started reaping the results of all my efforts. Now I can honestly say I earn my living as a writer. I am an author. But it did not happen overnight. My due season was over 31 years in length, but it came. Because I had planted, I am reaping.

The final, and in my opinion the most exciting, facet of the principle of recompense is that we will reap more than we sow! Again, this is illustrated in the physical world. If one grain of corn is planted—one seed—it grows into a stalk that contains several ears of corn with hundreds of kernels. Not a bad rate of exchange.

Solomon observed, "There is one who scatters, yet increases all the more. . . . The generous man will be prosperous" (Prov. 11:24,25). In other words, if we scatter "seeds" of righteousness, we will increase in righteousness, even though we are giving it away. In life, the way to reap a bountiful crop is to give of ourselves and our talents to others, and as we do we will prosper. We will get more than we give.

It would seem logical that if we want more of something we should keep it and add to it in some way, rather than turning loose of it; yet the Bible teaches that "he who sows sparingly shall also reap sparingly; and he who sows bountifully shall reap bountifully" (2 Cor. 9:6). This kind of philosophy is contrary to our human inclinations, but it works.

Christ exemplified the multiplicity factor when He laid down His life on the cross. In speaking of the results of His death, He reflected that, "Unless a grain of wheat falls into the earth and dies, it remains [just one grain; never becomes more but lives] by itself alone. But if it dies, it produces many others and yields a rich harvest" (John 12:24, *AMP*).

As an ultimate illustration of positive recompense, God sowed His only Son and in doing so reaped many other sons because, "As many as received [that precious, singular Son], to them He gave the right to become children of God" (John 1:12). By sacrificing one, He multiplied the number of His children by infinity. *We will reap more than we sow.* That is part of the joy of our reward, or conversely, the severity of our punishment.

Why, when this principle is so easy to understand, do so many of us refuse to use it to our advantage? Possibly it is because we see the truth that we will all face the consequences of our actions as a negative rather than a positive. Actually, it is a neutral and, as we have seen, we can control those consequences by doing what is morally right and good according to God's standards. Used properly, this principle is an insurance policy for easier living.

I think the main reason we do not aggressively use it for our betterment is because, although we want the benefits that result from the good we do, we do not want to accept the responsibility for the bad for our sin. So we try to ignore the idea of recompense altogether; to pretend we are not responsible for what happens to us when, to a great extent, we are.

Whether we like it or not, the principle of recompense carries with it the inherent burden of sowing what should be sown. Beyond that, it entails six basic responsibilities which, if we accept and act on them, will improve the quality of our lives and become a powerful force for our well-being.

Your Basic Responsibilities

1. You are responsible to accept the consequences for your actions. If you are going to be an emotionally healthy person, you must take control of your own life and be willing to get the credit for what you do or pay the piper. Many people wander through life blaming everyone and everything else for their misfortunes. Until you learn to say, "I did it and this is what happened," you will not be able to use the principle of recompense to your advantage because you will not see and eliminate your mistakes or identify and build on your strengths. "The wisdom of the prudent is to understand his way. . . . The backslider in heart will have his fill of his own ways, but a good man will be satisfied with his" (Prov. 14:8,14).

2. You are responsible to make proper choices. God created man with the right to choose. No one else can make you sin. The devil can't make you do it if you don't want to! If you do what is right, moral and loving you will reap the benefits of your choices. "A prudent man sees evil and hides himself, the naive proceed and pay the penalty" (Prov. 27:12). The choice is yours.

3. You are responsible to do your best. Man's way is to do as little as possible while short-cutting to get the most in return. Wisdom's way is to do your best; to work to the uttermost perimeter of your talents and abilities at all times so life can return to you in quality form. Slothfulness is self-destructive. "He who is loose and slack in his work is brother to him who is a destroyer [and he who does not use his endeavors to heal himself is brother to him who commits suicide]" (Prov. 18:9 *AMP*), but when you see someone who is skilled in his work, "He will stand before kings; he will not stand before obscure men" (Prov.22:29).

4. You are responsible to learn what you need to know. An old proverb sums it up this way, "Ignorance of the law is no excuse for breaking it." In other words, it is not acceptable for you to run a stop sign if you do not know you are supposed to stop. Similarly, it is not right for you to break God's moral standards and claim you did it because you do not know what they are.

The laws of life are not negated just because you do not know them. Life will not alter to suit your ignorance. Rather, you are responsible to learn what you need to know in order to live safely, securely and righteously. "It is not good for a person to be without knowledge" (Prov. 19:2). It may be downright dangerous. You must be responsible to educate yourself about God.

5. You are responsible for what you do to others. Cain's immortal question, "Am I my brother's keeper?" was a rhetorical one. You have a responsibility not to impinge upon the welfare of others and to consider how your actions will affect them. Remember, you will receive back in kind the blessing or the misery you bring into the lives of other people. If you try to make others happy, you will be happier. If you hurt them, you will be hurting yourself in some unseen way.

I am not inferring that you can be responsible for all the judgments and reactions others have toward you but I am saying that the law of recompense demands that if you purposely and knowingly misuse people, you will pay a price. "He who diligently seeks good seeks favor, but he who searches after evil, it will come to him" (Prov. 11:27).

6. You are responsible to act in good conscience. In the human sense, in the principle of reaping and sowing you are first and foremost accountable to yourself. When you are faced with a choice your criteria for judging what you should do should not be based on what others will think or what is in it for you, but solely on what is right. What you say and do must stand as pure in the eyes of God, be based on right motives and must leave you with a comfortable conscience. "He who walks blamelessly will be delivered, but he who is crooked will fall at once"; "To do righteousness and justice is desired by the Lord rather than sacrifice" (Prov. 28:18; 21:3). One major way to make your life easier is to live within the realm of moral responsibility.

Are you making good use of this important principle that God has built into His universe? You should be, by sowing righteousness and accepting your God-given responsibilities.

The law of recompense is operational at this very moment. It gives us the power to make our lives easier and less tumultuous by determining favorable results through our actions. We *will* reap what we sow. "The deeds of a man's hands will return to him" (Prov. 12:14).

Workshop

1. Using the chart, look up each Scripture reference in the first column. In the second column fill in what the verse says is sown and in the third column tell what is reaped. (Most verses will have two actions and results. The first one is an example.)

Reference	What Is Sown	What Is Reaped
3:35	*wisdom/foolishness*	*honor/dishonor*
10:2		
11:3		
11:17		
11:25		
12:13		
13:1		
13:11		
14:29		
15:18		
16:18		
17:9		
21:5		
23:20,21		

2. The following famous proverbs (not biblical) deal with the concept of recompense. Read each one, then write your interpretation, *as it applies to you,* in the space under each one. (The first one is an example.)

a. By work one comes to know the workman (LaFontaine). *What I do reflects my character and values.*

b. As you brew, so shall you bake (anon).

c. It is a poor heart that never rejoices (Charles Dickens).

d. If you cannot keep your own counsel, how can you expect another person to keep it? (anon)

e. Caution is the parent of safety (anon).

f. A rolling stone gathers no moss (Stephen Gosson).

g. The only way up is down (anon).

h. There are in nature neither rewards nor punishments; there are only consequences (Robert G. Ingersoll).

FOUR

Avoiding the Minus Factor

Do not enter the path of the wicked,
and do not proceed in the way of evil men; . . .
turn your foot from evil.
Proverbs 4:14,27

I knew when Brian came into the house, quietly sat down and looked innocent that he had been involved in something he shouldn't have. I asked him what was wrong.

"Nothing, really, Mom. I'm being good."

I nodded and asked him to tell me how he was being good. He proceeded to tell me that two other boys had taken some sneakers belonging to a neighbor girl and hidden them in the gutter. "They wanted me to do it too," he confessed, "but I said no and came in the house. I was turning my foot from evil," he concluded, quoting the Bible verse he had learned in Sunday School that week.

I tried not to laugh; he was so sincere and serious. I praised him for refusing to take part in the dire deed and told him how proud I was that he had done what the Lord would want him to do.

He beamed, then added a postscript. "But you know what, Mom? It sure wasn't easy."

It isn't easy to do what is right, to be faithful to God and obey His commandments; but it is beneficial and edifying. Yet, because we are weak, many times we let the minus factor of sin creep into our behavior patterns. Not only do such unrighteous actions subtract from godliness, but they complicate our lives and bring us worries and unnecessary misery.

Seduced by Sin

Why do we get trapped into doing wrong even when we want to do what is right? How does it happen? Why do we, as the apostle Paul lamented, "practice the very evil that (we) do not wish" (Rom. 7:19)? It is because we are wooed by and succumb to the charms of sin.

It follows, then, that if we can understand what sin is, how it entraps us and why we say yes to it instead of to God, we can avoid it and walk more consistently in the path of righteousness.

If we are going to elude the seductions of sin, we must understand exactly what sin is. We need to define it because each of us has our own definition. To one it may mean being disloyal, to another telling lies, to yet another cheating on the income tax or missing church on Sunday. *Webster's New World Dictionary* says sin is the breaking of religious law or a moral principle, through a willful act. While the wrongs we do are certainly a by-product of sin, they are not the sum and substance of it. In the overall sense, sin is rejecting God; defying who and what He is.

We also need to understand how we are ensnared by sin. In the book of Proverbs, sin, folly and man's wisdom are depicted as a prostitute—an adulterous woman or harlot who pulls people away from the path of righteousness. She entreats, woos and entices. Woo is an outdated term; it isn't

used much anymore. It means to court, coax, seek solici-
tously; to make love to.

How does sin capture and enamor us? It makes love to us!
It shows us only what we want to see, tells us only what we
want to hear, promises only what we want to happen. Literally, it seduces us; seeking to become our bedmate, our constant companion, a lover to whom we are devoted.

How does this seduction by sin actually transpire? And
why do we so easily fall prey to its enticement? The seventh
chapter of Proverbs depicts the wooing process and clearly
illustrates why we respond as readily as we do. Once we
study this passage of Scripture we should be better equipped
to withstand the charms of sin.

The story of the wooing process is told by a righteous
person, an observer who is watching someone become entrapped by sin. He tells us that when he was "at the window
of my house I looked out through my lattice" (Prov.7:6). We
see that this righteous witness has chosen to remain inside;
closeting himself in a safe place where he is protected and
sheltered from overt sin. He is not exposing himself to it.
Perhaps this is an example from the Holy Spirit, showing that
we must never purposely expose ourselves to evil. If we do,
we run the risk of becoming trapped in it.

The first thing the storyteller does is describe the kind of
people who are most susceptible to the drawing power of sin:
"I saw among the naive, I discerned among the youths, a
young man lacking sense" (Prov. 7:7). The naive are the
inexperienced who are easily led astray. They are not dis-
cerning. They just innocently accept everything at face value
and neither question nor critically judge what is proper and
correct. So, a person who is readily influenced by others or
circumstances, who responds without thinking or reasoning
through implications, can fall victim to sin. We must be
doubly careful of our responses, be cautious in determining
any line of conduct we choose to follow. We should be

certain that all of the decisions we make correspond with God's standards.

"Youth" was also present. Although this reference in Proverbs was about someone who was young in years, in a broader sense youth encompasses more than just age. It refers to someone who is not maturing spiritually; who is not learning God's Word or walking deeply with the Lord; who does not know God's principles of conduct or how to identify Satan when he attacks.

The particular youth which sin has singled out at the time of this story is described as "a young man lacking sense." He is not using his head, not thinking about what he is doing or where he is going. If he was, he would not be where he is—on a precarious, dangerous course. So we see that if we are naive, spiritually immature or thoughtless about our associates and associations, we can become prime targets for an attack by sin and will negligently surrender to evil's call.

We have to develop understanding, the ability to fully comprehend or perceive all opinions and facts which are presented to us. Because "discretion will guard you, understanding will watch over you, to deliver you from the way of evil" (Prov. 2:11,12).

Next we see that because this young man is not at all wise, he strays to the harlot. He wanders in her direction. "Passing through the street near her corner . . . he takes the way to her house, in the twilight, in the evening, in the middle of the night and in the darkness. And behold, a woman comes to meet him" (7:8-10). The fact that he was so easily enticed shows the danger of putting ourselves in the path of temptation.

Imagine his thought processes. He strolls along, passing *near* her corner, shrugs his shoulders and heads her way. The temptation is there, but as yet it is not sin. It is a neutral. How he handles it will dictate whether or not it becomes a transgression.

Subtleties of Sin

There is a subtle element here that may make it easier for the young man to give in to the temptation in which he has placed himself. It was twilight, sunset, when he took his first steps toward the house of the adulteress; but evidently he hung around for quite some time because he is still there many hours later, into the middle of the night.

It isn't difficult to see what happened. He toyed with temptation, flirted with wrongdoing. Eventually he talked himself into doing what he knew he shouldn't. We are not unlike this boy. More often than we care to admit we skirt the edge of respectability, tease ourselves with impurity and rationalize our behavior when we overstep the boundaries.

Another subtle consideration is that it was dark. If it had been daytime would he have been standing there? Probably not. He would not have wanted anyone to see him. But because there was no light he felt safe, protected. He may have been thinking, "No one will know if I give in." He sensed a safety in secrecy.

What can we learn from this? That we are more apt to sin if we think we won't get caught; if we can convince ourselves no one will know or find out. The problem with that line of reasoning is that God is light—it is His essence—so we can never hide from Him. There is no such thing as a secret sin where God is concerned. "The ways of a man are before the eyes of the Lord" (5:21).

As the young man is standing in the midst of temptation which he inflicted on himself, "a woman comes to meet him" (7:10). This woman is the harlot, the adulteress, the personification of wickedness. How did she know he was there? She was waiting for him! She was eager. She did not wait for him to come all the way to her. She went to meet him. Rest assured, she will do the same for us. Sin eagerly awaits our consent and will take any foothold it can get.

What is the harlot like? We are told she is "cunning of

heart . . . boisterous and rebellious" (7:10,11). Cunning of heart means it is her nature to be wily and deceitful; to harbor hidden motives and manipulative ploys.

This kind of subtlety has always been present in sin. The first thing we are told about the serpent, who came to tempt Eve, is that he "was more crafty than any beast of the field which the Lord God had made" (Gen. 3:1). And he was clever. He distorted what God had told Adam. God had instructed Adam, "From any tree of the garden you may eat freely; but from the tree of the knowledge of good and evil you shall not eat" (Gen. 2:16,17).

What did the serpent do? In the first sentence he uttered to Eve he chided her and put her on the defensive, saying, "Has God said, 'You shall not eat from *any* tree of the garden?' " (3:1, italics added). Next he distorted the truth. He convinced her that she would not die if she ate; that the only reason God didn't want her to learn about evil was because He did not want her to be like Him, "knowing good and evil" (3:5). He tantalized her by appealing to her pride. "*You* will be like God" (3:5, italics added).

His ploy worked. She ate the fruit and so did Adam. And when she ate she gained the knowledge of evil. Until that time she did not know what sin was so she was incapable of sinning. Imagine what it would be like not to know anything about sin. Wouldn't it be great? But, because Satan is cunning of heart and we are weak in the flesh, we do have that knowledge so we have to learn how to handle it; how to resist the wooing of sin.

Two other characteristics of sin that are described in this passage are that it is boisterous and rebellious. It is unruly, wild, uncontrolled, unrestrained. It runs rampant. Sin may be subtle but it is never subdued.

So the woman came to meet the young man. And what a greeting he received! He was warmly, passionately welcomed into open arms. "She seizes and kisses him" (Prov.

7:13). *Seize* means to grab hold of. She kissed him to evoke an emotional response, to make him feel desired and wanted.

What was the first thing the harlot said to her lover? "With a brazen face she says to him: 'I was due to offer peace offerings; today I have paid my vows. Therefore, I have come out to meet you' " (7:13-15). We see that the first thing she tells him is that she has performed her religious duties. She assures him that she has done what is right, what was required of her; she gave her offering and paid her vows.

Sound familiar? "I say my prayers." "I go to church." "I give my tithe." "I read the Bible." We only need to remember Jonestown to see that sin frequently disguises itself in the form of religious ritual. Formal religion is one of Satan's greatest weapons. If he can get people caught up in the form without the substance of godliness—the Person of Christ—he can keep them from the truth. Satan involves them in good works and rituals which, apart from Christ, are nothing. We must be certain it is the Lord Jesus Christ we are serving if we are going to understand and resist the wooing of sin.

Strength of Sin

Now let's analyze how the actual seduction occurs. The harlot is not coy or withdrawn—she comes on strong. Her attitude is brazen: bold, impudent, showing no shame or modesty. She is aggressive, and brashly propositions the young man. "I have come out to meet you, to seek your presence earnestly" (Prov. 7:15). So we find that sin appeals to us through an emotional attraction.

We must remember that as ugly as sin is—dark, dire and evil in nature—it comes in pretty packages. Sin always presents itself in ways that will elicit responses. We wouldn't be tempted if it was unattractive or repulsive. We'd mock a devil that wears a red suit, has horns and carries a pitchfork, but we succumb to one who is externally pleasant to look at and who flatters us and appeals to our pride.

Sin also appeals to us through our senses. The harlot seized and kissed her naive victim. She did what *felt* good, what stirred the emotions. She was dressed to attract the young man not necessarily in good taste but seductively. She set the scene by making the surroundings comfortable, pleasurable and sensual. "I have spread my couch with coverings, with colored linens of Egypt" (7:16)—an appeal to the sense of sight.

She did what appealed to the sense of smell: "I have sprinkled my bed with myrrh, aloes and cinnamon" (7:17). At this time it was believed that cinnamon was an aphrodisiac, a sexual stimulant that would arouse erotic responses. Aloes are sweet-smelling lilies, and myrrh is a delicately-scented perfume.

She also tantalized his senses of taste and touch. "Come, let us drink our fill of love until morning; let us delight ourselves with caresses" (7:18). She left nothing to chance—neither does sin.

Finally, the harlot seduced with words, appealing to the sense of hearing. "With her many persuasions she entices him; with her flattering lips she seduces him" (7;21). Notice that sin has *many* persuasions; a multitude of arguments to get us to give in to its wooing.

What are some of sin's verbal inducements? One is that no one will find out. The prostitute reassured the young man and calmed his guilt by telling him, "The man is not at home, he has gone on a long journey" (7:19). In other words, "Who will know?" That is one of Satan's favorite phrases. The truth is, God will. No one escapes His gaze. He is omnipresent. "The eyes of the Lord are in every place, watching the evil and the good" (Prov. 15:3).

Another lure sin uses is, "What will once matter?" Satan tries everything within his power to de-emphasize the severity of evil. He would like us to think that there are degrees of sin or that something is wrong only if we do it too often. But in God's sight, because He is holy, once does matter. Sin is sin. "He who turns away his ear from listening to the law, even his prayer is an abomination" (28:9). All sin, in any form, is intolerable to God.

A third way sin uses speech to wheedle us is by flattering us; it plays on our pride. The harlot "flatters with her words" (7:5) and has a "smooth tongue" (6:24). What she says swells our ego. She baits us by building a false sense of self-esteem. She chides us with phrases like, "Why should you listen to the pastor? He isn't going to tell you anything you don't already know." Or, "Why should you respect your husband? He's not nearly as spiritual as you are." Flattery!

So we see that sin appeals to us and woos us through our emotions and our physical senses. Satan will do anything he can to lower our resistance. And unless we are constantly on guard we will respond exactly as the young man did to the harlot: "Suddenly, he follows her" (7:22). He did not plan to give in. He didn't sit down and make a "List of Sins I Will Commit Today." He fell victim to an impulse!

He did not intend to yield to temptation but because he was where the temptation was, because he put himself in its path, *suddenly, he followed* and sin took him to bed.

Avoiding the Minus Factor

Once we realize how easily we respond to sin's wooing, how simple it is to get trapped by evil, we are better equipped to recognize it when it starts to draw us. But passive resistance is not enough. We need to aggressively avoid the minus factor of sin. Instead, we allow ourselves to be entrapped by default.

How can we escape being caught in sin's snare? A look at sin's wooing in the seventh chapter of Proverbs reveals there are six reasons why we become trapped. And in the fourth chapter, God gives us instruction through His servant, Solomon, concerning how we can resist unrighteousness. Let's look at each explanation of why we sin then examine the antidotes that will stave off the attacks.

Sin successfully woos us because we go where we should not. Remember, the young man strayed into doubtful territory. Scripture makes it extremely clear that there are two ways any of us can go, two paths, two routes: the path of righteousness or the path of unrighteousness. God issues two warnings. "Do not enter the path of the wicked, and do not proceed in the way of evil men" (Prov. 4:14).

First we are warned not to enter sin's path. If we don't take that first step, we will not be enticed. Secondly, we are cautioned not to proceed, which implies that even if we have started down the wrong path we can turn back. With God it is never too late. Sin cannot woo us if we are not in its way. The best protection is to stay away from it. Do not get involved in the first place.

Sin woos us because we expose ourselves to temptation. God tells us, "Avoid [sin], do not pass by it; turn away from it and pass on" (4:15). Avoiding means we take precautions not to go near it. I like to think that bypassing sin is a *divine detour* that God makes for our own protection and well-being. Detouring means taking the long way around if necessary. If we see a temptation we must literally turn and go the other way until it is removed. We may become intrigued by it if we get too close.

No matter how righteous we think we are, how morally strong, how able to resist, if we expose ourselves to temptation we are taking a perilous risk.

Sin successfully woos us because we respond through our senses, rather than acting on God's moral principles. Wicked men "eat the bread of wickedness, and drink the wine of violence" (4:17). When we partake of sin we internalize it as we do food and drink. We digest it. It saturates our system; it "gets into our blood"—becoming a part of our life force.

I do not want to give the impression that emotions are bad

or that it is wrong to feel deeply or to express our feelings. God created us with emotions sowe can experience life in the fullest sense. Feelings are not evil; it is the way we handle them that makes them unrighteous or righteous.

Eve is a classic example of someone who responded through her senses, rather that acting on God's moral principles. She "saw that the tree was good for food," and her appetite was stimulated. Both the tree and the fruit must have been beautiful: "it was a delight to the eyes." The mother of mankind probably reasoned that nothing that pretty could do much harm. Her pride was also involved: she knew that "the tree was desirable to make one wise" (Gen. 3:6).

So in the most cataclysmic act ever performed by a human being, "she *took* [touched] . . . its fruit and *ate* [tasted]" (Gen. 3:6). Eve looked, thought, took and ate. She did what felt and tasted good at the moment rather than obeying the Lord's command not to eat of the one tree. The same thing happens to us when we let our feelings control us. We look, think, take and taste evil without remembering what God requires of us.

Sin can also woo us when we are listening to it rather than to God. Perhaps that is why Solomon repeatedly admonishes us to listen carefully and thoughtfully to the Lord. He instructs us to "give attention to [wisdom's] words; incline your ear to [the Lord's] sayings" (Prov. 4:20).

Yet, how frequently we heed man's wisdom rather than God's. Man's ideas sound so good. They make sense to us. And they are what we want to do. That is why we must willfully ignore human desires when they conflict with the instruction of the Lord. We are responsible to "see to it that no one takes [us] captive through philosophy and empty deception, according to the tradition of men, according to the elementary principles of the world, rather than according to Christ" (Col. 2:8).

The Lord has only one perfect way—His will—for each

of us to respond to any situation. It is imperative we listen only to the wise. loving, heavenly Father.

Sin solicits favorable responses because it diminishes the light, dimming what is right and covering what is not. "The way of the wicked is like darkness" (Prov. 4:19). Like *darkness,* fearful, impenetrable, shutting out God's light and the warmth of His love.

How many of us when we sin are thinking about the Lord, envisioning Him watching us, reaching out to us? Don't we instead blot out all thought of Him and try to conceal our disobedience and the wrongs we do? We hide from His light and sneak into darkness to cover our sin.

When I was teaching a women's Bible study, I could always tell if someone was responding to sin's wooing because she would automatically and methodically gravitate toward darkness. First, she would stop preparing her lessons. Then she would become careless about studying. Next, she would start missing class, especially the prayer time. Finally, she would stop attending the group entirely and usually would not go to church anymore either. She was hiding from God's convicting light.

The only way to combat darkness is to overcome it with light. When you walk into a dark room at night you reach for the light switch. We must resist sin's wooing in the same way. Prayer, Bible reading and study, fellowship with God's people and open, honest confession must be such an intrinsic part of our lives that we call to the Lord, read His Word and lean on His people if we are tempted to turn from the light.

The final reason sin is victorious in our lives is because we choose to give in, even though we are taught that we should "Let [our] eyes look directly ahead, and let [our] gaze be fixed in front of [us]. Watch the path of [our] feet, and all [our] ways will be established. Do not turn to the right nor the left; turn [our feet] from evil" (Prov. 4:25-27).

We do not like to deal with the idea that when we sin it is

because we choose to, but the truth is that all sin is willful disobedience. God will not let us transgress accidentally. He sent Christ to save us from the power of sin. He supplied His Spirit to indwell those who believe in Him, and His Spirit is a *HOLY* Spirit—totally separate from all sin and evil. We are commanded to give full control of our lives to His holy essence; to be filled to overflowing with God. So we have no one but ourselves to blame if we are disobedient.

The only way to stop sinning is, by an act of the will, to halt. We are supposed to be following the Lord so we should focus our attention on Him; going only where He leads, not where we choose. "Let your eyes look directly ahead, and let your gaze be fixed straight in front of you" (Prov. 4:25), so all we see is the Lord who is leading us. Even a glance elsewhere can be dangerous, can lead us away from the path of righteousness.

We are to control where we look and where we walk. "Watch the path of your feet, and all your ways will be established" (4:26). We can get lost if we are not careful. We must watch our path to be sure we stay on the right road.

The only way to resist sin's wooing is to avoid the minus factor of sin. We must not: (1) go where we should not be; (2) expose ourselves to temptation; (3) respond through our senses; (4) listen to anyone but the Lord; (5) hide from His light or give in to the wooing. Rather we must constantly turn from evil and seek the Lord's will and way in our lives. We dare not "enter the path of the wicked," or "proceed in the way of evil men" (4:14).

Workshop

Read each of the proverbs listed here then write in your own words what is suggested that will help you turn your feet from evil and resist the wooing of sin.

Reference	Action
1:10	
1:15	
1:33	
2:20	
3:1	
3:7	
3:11	
3:21	
4:5,6	
4:13	
5:1	
7:1-5	
7:25	
8:33	
9:6	

FIVE

Watch What You Say!

Death and life are in the power of the tongue.
Proverbs 18:21

Each airline publishes a monthly magazine for its passengers to read. I was flipping through one when I was on my way to Philadelphia and a unique advertisement caught my eye. It was for a tongue cleaner. All that the user had to do was hook some sort of band around his tongue and pull down. This procedure was guaranteed to make one's mouth cleaner and fresher than it had ever been, and for only $3.98. I laughed when I read it, thinking that any device that could clean up a person's mouth would be a bargain at any price. It is something we could all use.

By the very nature of our society, all of us talk a great deal. We even tend to identify people by their speech patterns. We refer to someone as the strong, silent type or as a person of few words. Along more humorous lines, there's the old adage that if you want to spread some information all you need to do is telephone, telegraph or tell-a-woman. I recently heard someone who talks fast referred to as talking like she had been vaccinated with a phonograph needle.

Because of this abundance of verbal communication, it is only natural that our speech is a determining factor in our interpersonal relationships. And, because we talk so much and speaking is the most commonly used method of communication, usually we are not as thoughtful as we should be about what we say, how we say it, to whom we are saying it and how it will be received.

There isn't a person alive who hasn't gotten into trouble because of something he or she has said. I am convinced that a majority of our problems stem from remarks we make or the manner in which we say them. Careless speech causes numerous problems that can make life difficult.

Some speech problems are obvious but many of us have negative speech patterns of a more subtle variety that are not easily recognized. They are such a part of our character and emotional make-up that they go unnoticed. Life would be easier for many of us if we could isolate these problem areas and change our unsatisfactory speaking habits.

I am going to recommend a simple, three-step procedure I call the Three E's: *E*xamine, *E*xchange, and *E*liminate.

Examine your present speech patterns. This chapter is designed to help you do that.

Exchange bad speech habits for acceptable ones. Proverbs teaches us how to do that.

Eliminate unnecessary speech. Practice talking less and listening more.

The book of Proverbs is packed with wise hints that can help us implement the 3 E's. As I studied these I categorized the problems that are listed and the solutions that are offered. They are universal in nature and I know from my own experience that when I take them to heart, my life is easier. They can be used to evoke favorable responses from others, help us communicate more clearly, and keep us from being misunderstood or misquoted. In each instance we will look at the problem, then the scriptural solution.

Problem: Hasty Speech

Most of us are concerned more with saying what we have to say than we are with listening to the other guy. So we speak out of turn or before we should. Proverbs calls this "hasty speech." A hasty speaker shows one or more of these characteristics: he is defensive, argumentative, he lacks credibility, and he is rude and interruptive.

A person who is hasty to defend himself is warned to "not go out hastily to argue your case; otherwise, what will you do in the end?" (Prov. 25:8). Going out hastily to argue your case implies you are acting in an uncontrolled manner to defend yourself. You are being too defensive and argumentative. You prematurely protest and when the appropriate time comes for you to present your side of things, you don't have a case so your credibility is gone. Such a person exhibits three of the four characteristics.

I have seen parents make fools of themselves by hastily rushing out to defend and settle arguments between children. One incident I will never forget is when two families were yelling and shaking their fists at each other because the son of family number one had "socked" the daughter of family number two for cheating in a broomstick baseball game. As the parents were raging at each other, making all kinds of threats and accusations ("You borrowed my hammer and never returned it!" "Well, that should pay for all the cans of charcoal lighter you've taken and never returned!"), the kids sneaked off and started playing again. The whole incident was useless and happened because a father exploded when his daughter, who clearly outsized her supposed assailant, told him a boy had hit her and he ran out hastily to argue his case.

Interrupting is another characteristic of a hasty speaker. It is a listening defect that is based in pride. We do not want to hear what is being said to us because we are convinced that what we have to say is more meaningful and pertinent than what someone else is saying. Or, we think we know more and have more to contribute than someone else does, so we respond before another speaker has finished talking; we are compelled to answer before we have heard what the other person has to say.

One night I saw a woman lose $10,000 on a quiz show because she tried to out-guess what the question would be. She answered before the master of ceremonies had completed his sentence. It was a costly error because she heard only half of the question. The contestant grabbed her head and cried, "How could I have been so stupid?"

Interrupting others who are talking is extremely rude. It is a top-notch putdown. This particular symptom is common to married couples, where one will start to relate a story and the other will "sweetly" interrupt to correct a statement or add what he or she thinks is an important point.

What kinds of problems does hasty speech cause? Proverbs 29:20 observes, "Do you see a man who is hasty in his words? There is more hope for a fool than for him." People who listen to a person who is "hasty in his words" soon reject him. He loses credibility, and those who hear him will soon treat him as they would a fool. They discount what he says. He loses his audience.

A person who is quick to speak generally finds himself embarrassed because "he who gives an answer before he hears, it is folly and shame to him" (Prov. 18:13). There is very little good to say about one who is too hasty in speaking.

Solution: Guarded Speech

The proverbs offer a threefold solution to rapid, impulsive speech.

First, you should watch what you say, the content. "He who guards his mouth and his tongue guards his soul from troubles" (Prov. 21:23). *Guard* is a military term meaning to stand watch. When a soldier is on guard he is alert, watching for enemy forces that might unexpectedly invade his territory. He recognizes that unknown danger could be lurking in the background.

Guarding your speech means you will be on the alert for verbal patterns and habits which could cause you problems. Before you speak, you should be sure you can live with what you say after it is said. Choose words that will help, not hurt you and your listeners. Make what you are going to say pass mental inspection before you say it. Put your mind in gear before you put your mouth into motion.

Second, you need to watch the way you speak, your manner and attitude of presentation. "The heart of the righteous ponders how to answer, but the mouth of the wicked pours out evil things" (Prov. 15:28). Meditate about what you are going to say. Think about who will hear it, what your tone will imply and what you want to accomplish with your words. Ponder what you are going to say rather than blurt out whatever happens to be on your mind.

The opposite of pondering is pouring. During lunch the other day I shook the pepper shaker, expecting a few grains to fall onto my food. Instead, the entire shakerful of pepper tumbled into my salad. Needless to say, the food was ruined. The manager surmised that playful teenagers had purposely loosened the cap.

Poured words are like that poured pepper—carefully sifted speech seasons your life but indiscriminate words can ruin what is otherwise a good thing. God's standard is pondered speech; thoughtful words that season rather than destroy.

Third, you need to watch when you speak; guard your timing. "A man has joy in an apt answer, and how delightful is a timely word!" (Prov. 15:23). You need to watch for cues and learn timing in your speech, just as an actor has to listen for verbal signals from the rest of the cast so he will know when to speak. Saying the right thing at the right time in the right way is a cultivated art. You'll have to practice to perfect it.

Problem: Phony Speech

I know a woman who is one of the sweetest, most unassuming people I have I have ever met but she has a habit of calling everybody "dahling." Because of this, many people assume she is a phony. Although most of us don't run around calling people "dahling," we have incorporated similar superficial techniques into our vocabularies.

Phony speech comes packaged in two ways: as facetiousness or as flattery. A person who speaks facetiously is usually saying one thing when he means the opposite. He calls it joking or teasing but it is the parent of many difficulties because people cannot determine when you are serious about what you are saying and when you are not. Actually, facetiousness is a form of deceit and is impossible to interpret correctly.

Proverbs 26:18,19 stresses the dangers of this type of insincere speech. "Like a madman who throws firebrands, arrows and death, so is the man who deceives his neighbor, and says, 'Was I not joking?' " The implication is that, just as a madman wildly fires a gun or uses explosives, and wounds and hurts people at random, so does a person who jokes or teases.

I do not believe this means you should not laugh and have fun but rather that you must be careful not to misuse your humor, especially at someone else's expense. The apostle Paul admonishes that "there must be no filthiness and silly talk, or *coarse jesting*" (Eph. 5:4, italics added).

Facetiousness can cause all kinds of problems. What is

spoken as a joke may be received as a fact and mistrust will result. I once jokingly remarked to a friend, who understood what I was saying, that I had told George he could either shape up or ship out. Someone overheard and the next thing I knew there was rumor circulating that the Berrys were having marriage problems and I had asked my husband to move out! *No silly talk!*

We went to a concert this summer and during his performance, the star conversed with people in the audience. One was a woman who had idolized him for many years. She told him how she had always wanted to meet him, how handsome he still was and how she had been in love with him simce she was 13. The singer wisecracked, "I guess I better see you in my dressing room backstage after tonight's performance."

As George, Brenda and I were walking out we noticed that poor woman standing by the stage stairs, anxiously waiting to go backstage. She had taken her idol's remark literally. I wonder how long it was before the disillusionment set in? *No coarse jesting!*

Another form of phony speech is flattery. Flattery is telling people what you think they want to hear so you can get what you want from them. It is a form of manipulation. The dictionary defines *manipulate* as: to tamper with, manage by crafty means or to direct unethically. It is the opposite of sincere, honest persuasion.

More of us are more guilty of this than would care to admit. You want Ann to assist in children's church because you have to get the roster filled, so you tell her what a great organizer she is and how wonderful she is with kids. Or, Lois coos to Marie about the "be-you-tee-ful" dress she's wearing because she needs her to serve as an officer on the women's board.

Flattery is hypocrisy put into words and is volatile because it can backfire. "A man who flatters his neighbor is spreading a net for his steps. . . . A flattering mouth works ruin" (Prov.29:5; 26:28). You will hurt both yourself and others if you indulge in phony speech. You will ruin relationships and get trapped in a verbal web of deceit, thereby complicating your life.

Solution: Persuasive Speech

The opposite of facetiousness and flattery is persuasive speech, which is characterized by sincerity and potency. A persuasive speaker employs words that are both guileless and powerful. He knows how to *state* his case in a convincing way, *present* facts that are free from innuendo, openly *share* his opinion, and *explain* why he believes as he does.

Learning to talk this way is not easy. It is a learned response. "The heart of the wise teaches his mouth, and adds persuasiveness to his lips" (Prov. 16:23). Apparently, you must teach yourself how to speak in a straightforward manner. So instead of flattering Ann to get her to assist in children's church, you should tell her how much you need her help and give honest reasons why you think she would be good in that position. Lois should explain to Marie that she needs her particular kind of expertise to complete the women's board rather than fussing over her dress, which is not a part of the issue.

Persuasive speech is also characterized by power. A person who knows how to use words wisely and well is listened to and usually accomplishes what he wants to accomplish. I love the story about the time Henrietta Mears, that great Christian teacher who emulated the Master's ability to handle her vocabulary with both tact and power, was visiting the Taj Mahal in India. "Her guide, in order to prove the unusual acoustics of the high-domed structure, stood on the platform in the center of the main hall and shouted: 'There is no God but Allah, and Mohammed is his prophet!' His cry rang sonorously through all the chambers of the monument.

"Then Doctor Mears asked if she too might say something, and when permission was granted, she ascended the steps and proclaimed in her low, powerful voice: 'Jesus Christ, Son of God, is Lord over all!' Like peals of thunder rolling through the canyons and across the valleys of an alpine mountain range, her words raced from wall to wall and down the corridors of the minareted shrine: 'Lord over all, over all, over all!' "[1] *That* is persuasive speech.

Problem: Gossip

Another, and probably the most common speech problem is gossip. Would you call yourself a gossip? If you define gossip the way most people do—as nasty, malicious, pointedly hurtful talk—then you probably do not think of yourself as one. A look in the dictionary reveals the many faces of gossip. It defines *gossip* as groundless rumor, hearsay, idle talk, prating and chatting needlessly.

The book of Proverbs refines this further by showing that gossip is *talebearing*—repeating stories, rumors or secrets—and also *slandering* and *talking too much*. Now, in light of those definitions could you be labeled a gossip? In some way the name fits us all, doesn't it? To overcome the problem of gossip you must recognize how insidious and harmful it is and what it involves.

One thing gossip embodies is bearing tales. "He who goes about as a talebearer reveals secrets" (Prov. 11:13). So gossip is running around telling stories; "going about" hearing something and purposely choosing to spread it. It is betraying both implied and stated confidences. (Which one of us hasn't at some time heard a juicy story and waltzed to the phone to relay it to someone?)

Gossip also involves revealing secrets; and whether they are betrayed accidentally or on purpose is irrelevant. A confidence is broken, a privacy disclosed, a breach of trust occurs. Relationships, even close-knit ones, can be damaged or destroyed when information is repeated. "He who repeats a matter separates *intimate* friends" (Prov. 17:9, italics added). Notice that it is "a matter" that is repeated. Neither the quality nor the veracity of the facts nor the intent of the speaker is the issue. The damage is in the speaking. It is destructive to say something you have no right to say.

I know of an instance when a wife shared some intimate, unflattering truths about her and her husband's sex life at a women's Bible study that was dealing with the topic of the sexual relationship in marriage. She did it thoughtlessly, asking questions and making remarks like, "But my husband always . . ." Unfortunately, the class was taped and the husband heard the tape and it almost caused a divorce.

Along with bearing tales—going about repeating matters and revealing secrets—*gossip incorporates slander:* purposely and maliciously speaking against others. I assume that most of you who read this book will not fall into that category, but quite possibly you might know someone who does. We are admonished that, "He who goes about as a slanderer reveals secrets, therefore, *do not associate with a gossip*" (Prov. 20:19, italics added). The godly warning is *do not associate!* We should not even expose ourselves to such people lest we be judged guilty by association or pick up their unseemly behavior patterns.

Finally, gossip entails doing what comes naturally to most of us—talking too much. Overtalking is dangerous because, "When there are many words, transgression is unavoidable" (Prov. 10:19). It is a fact of life that if you talk too much inevitably you will say the wrong thing. The more you say, the more you let down your guard, the easier it is to sin with your mouth. If you talk too much you will make trouble for yourself.

Solution: Restraint and Silence

Obviously, the way to stop gossiping is not to talk *about*

others *to* others. Sometimes people in my classes say, "But if we believed that all those things are gossiping, we'd never talk." My reply is, "No, we would still talk but we would talk a lot less and with much discretion."

Like it or not, silence is one infallible solution to the problem of gossip. In "Meditations," Pineart said, "For each sin which we may commit by keeping silence where it would be well to speak, we commit a hundred by speaking up on all occasions." In other words, we get in trouble much more frequently for what we say rather than for not speaking up when we should.

Because we like to talk and it is enjoyable to us, we do not value silence. Silence is a form of understanding. Solomon observed that, "A man of understanding keeps silent" (Prov. 11:12). I remember when my father died, I felt like screaming at all of the people who were huddling over me, trying to console me with words. But when my two best friends came to the house we just went into my bedroom and sat for hours without saying a word. Why? Because they understood, they kept silent.

Silence also cloaks our faults and stupidities and keeps us from making verbal mistakes. "Even a fool, when he keeps silent, is considered wise; when he closes his lips, he is counted prudent" (Prov. 17:28). Your ignorance, your prejudices, your inadequacies show when you speak. Rather than risking getting in over your head, if you keep quiet and respond only when you must, you will appear to be wise and knowledgeable even if you are not. Why not be good to yourself and try saying less?

If you are going to eliminate the problem of gossip and cultivate the creativity of silence, you need to go on a *word diet*. A word diet is much like a food diet. Basically a diet involves cutting down on how much you eat and limiting your intake of foods to those that are nonfattening and nutritious. Likewise, a word diet involves cutting down on the quantity of your words—saying less—and improving the quality of your words.

A word diet consists of two don'ts and four dos. The don'ts are: (1) don't speak until you have thought about what you will say—evaluate the content; (2) don't speak until you have thought about the effect of what you will say—evaluate the results. The dos are: (1) do purposely try not talking when you badly want to—weigh the benefits of silence versus speech—does it need to be said? (2) Do use nonverbal communication—smile, frown, nod or shake your head, look puzzled, take someone's hand, instead of speaking; (3) do state positives before negatives—if you save the worst until last you might not say it at all; (4) do undertalk—say as little as possible; become a man or woman of fewer words.

The other solution to gossip is to use restraint when you speak. "He who restrains his words has knowledge, and he who has a cool spirit is a man of understanding. . . . He who restrains his lips is wise" (Prov. 17:27; 10:19). Restrained speech means holding back with what you say; picking and choosing your words rather than blurting them out; understating rather than over-explaining. Restraint means you control your mouth.

For example, I have a husband who is a master at one-line comebacks. Where I would reply to someone with several paragraphs, he answers in a phrase. He never reacts verbally until he has thought about what has been said and what he is going to say. Consequently, when he does talk, everybody listens. They know when George speaks he has something worth saying. Such restraint!

Restraint is also refusing to contribute to gossip. We have already noted that it is foolish to associate with a gossip but how can you control yourself in social situations? Some helpful methods are:

1. Don't listen to gossip. Sometimes we feel it would be rude to leave a gossip session. Not so. Gossiping is

impolite. Not listening is courteous, safe and smart. Walk
away. Excuse yourself and go.

2. State your feelings. Say you would prefer not to hear what
   is being said.
3. Change the subject. Move to safer ground.
4. Make positive statements in response to negative ones.
5. Call it what it is. Simply say you believe what you are
   hearing is gossip.

A subtle but inherent danger you face when you listen to
gossip is that you run the very real risk of hearing something
you will not want to hear or learning something you do not
want or need to know. When you listen, you are accountable
for what you hear.

I will never forget the time I inadvertently found out,
when I was having lunch with a group of women, that the
husband of one of my close friends was involved with
another woman. I hated hearing that. I did not want to know
it. I was forced to decide what to do with the information and
agonized hundreds of times about how much better, simpler
and easier it would have been for all of us if I had never
known. I desperately wished I hadn't heard about it because
when I did I became responsible for what I knew. The wisest
way to avoid gossip is don't do it or listen to it.

Making the Exchange: Good for Bad

In Ephesians 4:29, Paul gives four qualifications of restrained speech, standards you can use as you exchange your
old speech patterns for acceptable ones. He instructs us to,
"Let no unwholesome word proceed from your mouth, but
only such a word as is good for edification according to the
need of the moment, that it may give grace to those who
hear."

First, what you say must be wholesome, be of some
value, have a richness, some redeeming quality.

Second, what you say must build up, not destroy. Even

negatives should be stated in uplifting ways and your motive for speaking them should be to edify the listener. The biblical meaning of the word edify is "to take to the highest pinnacle." Your words should be a positive, elevating force.

Third, what you say must need to be said when you say it. It must be needful for the moment. When your son calls to say he ran out of gas five blocks from the house, it is not the time to remind him he should have stopped at the filling station on his way home. When your daughter gets a D on her algebra test it isn't the time to tell her she should have studied harder. If someone is not ready or willing to listen, or if you would merely be saying "I told you so," what you say is not needful. Needful words make a positive contribution.

Fourth, what you say must give grace to those who hear. It should contribute to their happiness, be worth repeating and be said with the proper tone. And, it should be pleasing to anyone who accidentally overhears.

This poem from the Arabian beautifully summarizes what we have been discussing.

Three Gates

If you are tempted to reveal
A tale to you someone has told
About another, make it pass
Before you speak, three gates of God.
These narrow gates:
First, is it true?
Then, is it needful?
In your mind give truthful answer.
And the next is last and narrowest:
Is it kind?
And if to reach your lips at last
It passes through these gateways three,
Then you may tell the tale,
Not fearing what the result may be.

Remember, your speech is a reflection of your soul and reveals you to others. "Life and death *are* in the power of the tongue" (see Prov. 18:21). If you realize the force your words can have, life will be easier.

Workshop

1. Is hasty speech one of your problems? Rate yourself to see where improvement is needed. Use N for *never;* S for *sometimes;* U for *usually;* A for *always.*

	N	S	U	A
a. I speak defensively on my own behalf.	☐	☐	☐	☐
b. I find I must consistently explain myself to others.	☐	☐	☐	☐
c. What I say is easily understood.	☐	☐	☐	☐
d. I am argumentative.	☐	☐	☐	☐
e. Others listen when I talk.	☐	☐	☐	☐
f. I am a good listener.	☐	☐	☐	☐
g. I interrupt when others are talking.	☐	☐	☐	☐
h. I think about what I am going to say before I speak.	☐	☐	☐	☐
i. I think about who will hear me before I speak.	☐	☐	☐	☐
j. I think about the consequences of my words before I say them.	☐	☐	☐	☐

2. Some famous proverbs about speech are listed here.

Read each one and write your interpretation of it, as it applies to you, in the spaces below.

    a. A bird is known by its note, a man by his talk (anon.).

    b. You may blot out what is written but what is spoken can never be recalled (Horace).

    c. Be silent or say something better than silence (anon.).

    d. Silence is a still noise (Josh Billings).

    e. Little said is soonest mended (George Wither).

    f. Discretion in speech is more than eloquence (Francis Bacon).

    g. The true use of speech is not so much to express our wants as to conceal them (Oliver Goldsmith).

    h. Speech is the index of the mind (Seneca).

    i. Silence and modesty are very valuable qualities in conversation (Michel de Montaigne).

    j. Words, like eyeglasses, blur everything that they do not make more clear (Joseph Joubert).

k. Give a gracious word a host of tongues but let ill tidings tell themselves (Shakespeare).

l. Sarcasm is an insult in dress suit (anon.).

m. He approaches nearest to the gods who knows how to be silent even though he knows he is right (Cato).

n. And 'tis remarkable that they talk most that have least to say (Prior).

3. Look up each verse from Proverbs then fill in the chart. Some verses may have more than one answer.

Reference	Type of Speech	Action
4:24		
10:31		
10:32		
11:9		
11:12		
13:17		
14:3		

Reference	Type of Speech	Action
15:4		
15:23		
16:30		
17:4		
21:23		
24:1,2		

Note

1. Ethel May Baldwin and David V. Benson, *Henrietta Mears and How She Did It* (Ventura, CA: Regal Books, 1966).

SIX

The Truth of the Matter

The Lord hates . . . a lying tongue.
Proverbs 6:16,17

I was excited about attending the luncheon because an internationally known speaker was delivering the keynote address. During the course of her talk she told a story to illustrate the character of God, and she told it as if it had happened to her husband, his personal experience. She said her husband observed these events a few months before while they were moving into their house. I happened to know thay had been married about two years at that time.

It was a potent analogy, beautifully reflective of God's nature; but there was a problem with it. I had heard the same story at least six years before when a friend of mine used it to illustrate a point in the Bible study. The difference was, she had not told it as if it had happened to her personally.

As I sat there, I remember thinking, "The speaker is

lying. That didn't happen to her husband just a few months ago. That analogy has been circulating in Christian circles for quite some time." Then I tried to justify why she had "stretched the truth." Maybe she wanted to make the point more personal. Perhaps she was repeating it the way she had heard it and just stuck her husband's name in. Or she simply didn't realize she was being untruthful.

But try as I might, I heard very little else she had to say. She had been less than candid and her message was lost to me. In my eyes, she didn't have credibility.

Certainly, I am not sitting in judgment on her. I dare not because all of us are guilty of the sin of lying. We may do it purposely or, as that woman, unintentionally, but *all of us lie,* probably more frequently than we think or notice. It is an incorporated part of our old sin nature.

I'm sure your first reaction to that observation is, "I am *not* a liar." True, untruthfulness may or may not be an ongoing behavior pattern in your life; you may not be habitually untruthful. But no matter how honest any of us are, we all lie, and the lies we tell (or the truth we withhold) complicate our lives and are immeasurably harmful. If we are going to live the kind of harmonious, guilt-free lives God intended, then we need to admit to this frailty of character and discover what we can do to eliminate it.

What Is a Lie?

If I asked you to write your definition of a lie, you would probably say it is telling an untruth. That is one kind of lie, but as we will see, there are many types, and telling a falsehood is only one of them. In a broad, general sense, *a lie is any form of untruth,* thought or acted out in word or deed.

Those of us who think of ourselves as honest should be aware that the deeper our Christianity is, the more subtle this sin will be. No one who is committed to the Lord, who is trying to walk the path of righteousness, lies consistently or overtly. We are not barefaced liars, but we skirt the fringes of fidelity. We hear a story and repeat it without verifying the facts. We exaggerate to make a point. We lie in subtle ways.

Frequently we excuse our fabrications by saying that lying is not always a sin, that we must be truthful and take care not to hurt people's feelings. And that is true. But is lying synonymous with tact and sensitivity? As much as we wish it were, it is not. Being tactful doesn't mean we have to lie: it is "speaking the truth in love" (Eph. 4:15). In other words, there is a right way and a wrong way to state the truth. When we do "speak the truth" we should be motivated by love and not embellish the facts.

Proverbs 6:16,17 lists seven sins that the Lord hates. Five of them involve some form of prevarication and one of them, pride, is the cause of our untruthfulness. "There are six things which the Lord hates, yes, seven which are an abomination to Him: haughty eyes, a lying tongue, and hands that shed innocent blood, a heart that devises wicked plans, feet that run rapidly to evil, a false witness who utters lies, and one who spreads strife among brothers."

Our arrogance makes us lie. We want to be liked, be accepted, get our own way, exalt ourselves at the expense of others, defend our perfect opinions, cover our tracks, make a point—so we lie. We devise—plant and plan—lies in our heart. When we gossip, we are only too glad to quickly tell a story about another—our feet *do* run rapidly to evil. A false witness does not tell the truth when it is within his power to do so, and lies certainly do spread strife among brothers. Deception is divisive.

Solomon says these verbal sins are an *abomination* to the Lord. Exactly what does that mean? When something is an abomination to us it means we have a sickening dislike for it. It is both emotionally and physically repulsive. That is God's response to falsehood. So I would say we can assume that since all lies are intolerable to Him, they are always wrong.

There is another reason lying is wrong. God is truth. The truth is not something He tells, it is part of His essence. We say there is nothing God cannot do, that He is omnipotent. And He is, yet Scripture teaches that "it is impossible for God to lie" (Heb.6:18), that "[His] mouth will utter truth; and wickedness is an abomination to [His] lips. All the utterances of [His] mouth are in righteousness; there is nothing crooked or perverted in them" (Prov. 8:7,8). God's power is seen in the fact that He does not lie.

Christ taught that "God is spirit; and those who worship Him must worship in spirit and truth" (John 4:24). So any fib, no matter how small in our estimation, is an affront to God's attribute of truth.

Source of Lies

If we belong to the Lord and God is truth, why do we lie? We lie when we focus off of the Lord and onto ourselves, concentrating on what we want and how to get it rather than on who God is. We use our tainted, human resources for getting things rather than relying on God to supply us out of His grace.

The Bible teaches that there are two sources of falsehood. One is *our own human soul,* our heart. "The heart is more deceitful than all else" (Jer. 17:9). We fool ourselves by inventing proper motives for our improper actions. We always say, "I lied because," and have what we consider a gallant reason for doing it. We deceive ourselves.

Satan, our spiritual adversary, is the other source of lies. Jesus taught that the devil "does not stand in the truth, because there is *no* truth in him. Whenever he speaks a lie, he speaks from his own nature; for he is a liar, and the father of lies" (John 8:44, italics added). Just as God's essence is truth, Satan's essence is falsity. There is *no* truth in him. Everything he does is based in deceit. It is his nature, his total inclination to lie.

He is the source, the father of lies. He impregnates our minds and souls with his prevarications, conceives our falsehoods, then brings them to fruition in what we agree to say and do when we are tempted. Anytime we lie, Satan is behind it.

I'll be honest. I don't like dealing with the fact that I lie and that all lies are sin, an affront to the holy essence of God. But if I am to believe God's Word then I must act on that premise; and this creates a dilemma for me, and for any of us who want to keep the entire counsel of the Lord. Knowing how and why we lie will help us understand our inclination to fabricate. As we broaden our understanding of what falsehood is, we will be able to spot and eliminate it in our behavior.

God is so gracious. He has peppered the pages of the Bible with vivid portraits of how His saints, right along with unbelievers, misuse the truth. He warns us about the dangers of lying and at the same time encourages us by showing us that we are not alone, that His people down through the ages have had this problem but have gone on to victorious, righteous living.

Paul noted that, "Whatever was written in earlier times was written for our instruction, that through perseverance and the encouragement of the Scriptures we might have hope" (Rom. 15:4). So even though we lie, deceive ourselves and embroider the truth, there is hope for us. We are not a lost cause. Dishonesty can be conquered!

Kinds of Lies

If we are going to overcome our tendency to lie we must fully comprehend what lying is; grasp the full scope of untruthfulness. A close examination of the Scriptures reveals that falsehood falls into eight general categories: (1) lies of commission, (2) lies of omission, (3) perjury, (4) gossip/slander, (5) exaggeration, (6) manipulation, (7) hypocrisy, and (8) faithlessness. We need to define each type and see where our shortcomings are in regards to deceptiveness.

The first kind of untruth is the lie of commission: telling something that is not true and implying, stating or inferring that it is. We do not need to read far in the pages of Scripture to find the first lie of this kind. In Genesis 3:4, Satan assured Eve that if she disobeyed God and ate from the tree of the knowledge of good and evil that no harm would befall her. "You surely shall not die." A blatant lie.

In the very next chapter, Cain, after he had killed Abel, boldly lied to God. "The Lord said to Cain, 'Where is Abel your brother?' And he said, 'I do not know' " (Gen. 4:9). Likewise, Sarah also lied to the Lord. When God told Abraham that he and Sarah would conceive a child the idea seemed so ridiculous to her that she laughed to herself. The Lord, being able to read her heart, asked, "Why did Sarah laugh?" And, "Sarah denied it . . . saying, 'I did not laugh'; for she was afraid" (Gen 18:13,15).

What motivated these lies of commission? We have already seen that Satan lies because it is his nature. But it appears that both Cain and Sarah lied because they had done something they should not have and they wanted to cover it up. They were afraid of being discovered, of being caught in their sin, so they compounded their transgressions by lying.

An equally common kind of misrepresentation is the lie of omission. This comes in two forms: (1) not telling the truth when we should or (2) telling only partial instead of complete truth. We omit important facts when they should be included. Or we do not know the whose truth but we repeat what we do know, thereby leaving out the crucial data.

Abraham, the father of our faith, was guilty of this kind of equivocation. In the twentieth chapter of Genesis, we read that he, for some unknown reason, passed Sarah off to King Abimelech as his sister. And that was not exactly a lie. At least, it was almost true; she was his half-sister, the daughter of his father but not of his mother (see Gen. 20:12). The problem was he omitted one important detail: Sarah was also his wife.

God mercifully kept Abimelech from committing sexual sin with Sarah, but the king was indignant when he discovered he had been lied to. He rebuked Abraham, saying, "You have done to me things that ought not to be done" (Gen. 20:9). No one deserves to be deceived.

Another kind of lie is perjury: being a false witness, not attesting to the truth when it is in our power to do so; lying about what is true or making false accusations. Remember, a false witness is included in the list of seven abominable sins.

Our Lord was subjected to this kind of judicial mistreatment. "Now the chief priests and the whole Council kept trying to obtain false testimony against Jesus, in order that they might put Him to death; and they did not find it, even though many false witnesses came forward" (Matt. 26:59,60).

Perjury is not just morally wrong; it is a crime. Even in today's permissive society, lying on the witness stand is punishable by imprisonment. Why? Because it thwarts the entire justice system. It lets the guilty go free and convicts the innocent. Because of this, anyone who testifies in court is asked to take an oath concerning the veracity of his testimony and is warned that he will be liable if he withholds the truth or tells a lie.

Being a false witness does not apply only in a courtroom. Anytime we give untrue testimony about anything or anybody we are being false witnesses. We are not to make false accusations against anyone, ever. The Lord commands us, "Do not be a witness against your neighbor without cause, and do not deceive with your lips" (Prov. 24:28). He promises that "a false witness will not go unpunished" (Prov. 19:5).

I am certain most of us would not lie on the witness stand

but if one facet of being a false witness is withholding truth, does that not emphasize the necessity of our coming forth with information that may help absolve someone of quilt or clear a name or reputation? God has commanded that we are not to "withhold good from those to whom it is due, when it is in [our] power to do it" (Prov. 3:27). We live in a time when people are reluctant to get involved, yet God's Word is quite explicit that we must practice being true witnesses in the fullest sense.

Being a false witness in any matter is detrimental because it makes the truth look like a lie. Being a truthful witness is speaking what we sincerely *believe* is true. There is no way any of us can always have complete, objective information, so God asks us to state the agreement between our convictions and our consciences; that we utter only what we are convinced is literally true.

The fourth kind of lie is gossip and slander; the accidental or purposeful, malicious telling of untruths or private matters; the illicit spreading of information. When we gossip we run the risk of slandering someone. If we tell unverified facts, not knowing whether they are true or not, or when we misquote someone, we are slandering them. Slander is making false statements that defame a person's character.

Remember the old parlor game "gossip"? Several people sit in a circle and whoever is "it" whispers a sentence to the person next to him. He can only say it once. That person then whispers it to the next, and so on, until it reaches the last one in the circle. That last person repeats aloud the message as he received it. It is comical to see how an innocent sentence can get so distorted in the telling.

Because this kind of distortion happens so easily, gossip many times evolves into slander even if we do not intend to malign a person. Sadly, there are people in this world who knowingly will assassinate someone's character in order to get what they want or to seek revenge.

Joseph was the victim of this kind of verbal attack. When Potiphar's wife tried to seduce him, to the point of tearing his clothes off his back, and he rejected her, she accused him of attempted rape and he was thrown into prison (see Gen.39:12-20). We need to remember that anger and rejection can make us do strange, sinful things.

Exaggeration is another form of lying. It is overstating the truth, bragging or boasting, flattering others with excessive, and sometimes undeserved, praise. Eve fell prey to exaggeration when she was talking to the serpent. He baited her by asking if God had forbidden her and Adam to eat of *any* tree in Eden and when she answered she added a detail of her own, just to make the story a little better. She said, "From the fruit of the trees of the garden we may eat; but from the fruit of the tree which is in the middle of the garden, God has said, 'You shall not eat from it *or touch it*' " (Gen. 3:2,3).

God had not told them not to touch the fruit, merely not to eat it. But to make her point Eve stretched the truth and Satan capitalized on her verbal error.

I think that probably more than any other form of dishonesty many of us are guilty of this. We say 500 when it's 368. We say many when we mean several. We say we have a terrible headache when there is only a slight throb. We "butter up" people to get things from them. We slant the story to make ourselves look good.

I must admit there was a time when I was an inveterate exaggerator. Being a writer, I am also a storyteller, and I would add little touches to "spice up" the content. I finally learned my lesson when I was teaching about this topic at a women's retreat and I told a story about a dog we'd had who (I said) dug holes 10 feet deep in our backyard. The audience roared with laughter. They thought I had purposely exaggerated, but I did it accidentally, out of habit. So there I was, teaching against this kind of sin and doing it as I taught.

Christ, our example, said, "I have been born, and for this

I have come into the world, to bear witness to the truth" (John 18:37). As His witnesses we have an obligation to be accurate, even in small things. Slight inaccuracies may not seem important but they open the door for more gross forms of deceit. Hedging in minor areas can create within us an indifference to know all the facts, and pretty soon we are desensitized to the need for exactness, so it doesn't matter to us if we tell a lie here or there.

Society has coped with exaggeration by making rules that allow for it. For instance, we believe it is wrong to tell a "big black lie"—I should not tell you I make $50,000 a year if I make only $5,000. But "little white lies" are permitted. Therefore, I can say I make $60,000 if I make only $50,000. And it is easy for us to fall in line with this mentality unless we do battle against it.

We must not exaggerate to stress our own importance but, "let another praise you, and not your own mouth; a stranger, and not your own lips" (Prov. 27:2). We should sift our words carefully before we say them, making certain there are no added fictions. If our speech is sincere and without guile we will maintain our integrity and "better is a poor man who walks in his intergrity than he who is perverse in speech and is a fool" (Prov. 19:1).

Manipulation with words or body language, twisting the truth and the way it is presented is another type of lying. This kind of fraudulent influence is particularly insidious because it undermines the trust one person places in another. Manipulation is a way of using people for personal advantage.

This form of deceit is vividly portrayed in Genesis 27 when Rebekah and Jacob take advantage of Isaac, who is physically feeble and almost blind. They tricked Isaac into believing that Jacob was Esau by disguising Jacob with a goatskin covering, so he could steal his brother Esau's birthright.

This manipulation of a beloved husband and father was

treacherous. Rebekah instructed Jacob to prepare Isaac's favorite food and bring it to him, pretending to be Esau. " Go now to the flock and bring me from there two choice kids, and I will prepare them a savory dish for your father, such as he loves. Then you shall bring it to your father, that he may eat, so that he [will think you are Esau and] may bless you before his death" (Gen.27:9,10).

This incident also involved betrayal of trust. Jacob feared that his father would know it was him and not Esau. "Jacob answered his mother Rebekah, 'Behold, Esau my brother is a hairy man and I am a smooth man. Perhaps my father will feel me, then I shall be as a deceiver in his sight; and I shall bring upon myself a curse and not a blessing' " (Gen. 27:11,12). He wasn't concerned that he was deceiving his father or how hurt Isaac would be, he was concerned only for himself—that he not get caught and get into trouble.

But Rebekah took care of that problem too, and in doing so betrayed her own husband. She "took the best garments of Esau her elder son, which were with her in the house, and put them on Jacob her younger son. And she put the skins of the kids on his hands and on the smooth part of his neck" (Gen. 27:15,16).

Their ploy also involved telling outright, planned lies. When Jacob approached his father with the food and spoke to him the old man suspected it was not Esau who was with him. He said, "The voice is the voice of Jacob, but the hands are the hands of Esau" (v. 22). Then he asked Jacob, "Are you really my son Esau?" and Jacob said, "I am" (v. 24). And after Isaac blessed him, he embraced and kissed his son. How must Jacob have felt?

Great harm came from this deceit. When Isaac learned the truth he "trembled violently" (v. 33). Esau "cried out with an exceedingly great and bitter cry" (v. 34) and "bore a grudge against Jacob because of the blessing with which his father had blessed him; and Esau said to himself, 'The days of mourning for my father are near; then I will kill my brother Jacob' " (v. 41).

Our manipulations may not be as well-planned as Rebekah's and Jacob's, but sometimes we also try to manage our circumstances by crafty means rather than using straightforward communication. Manipulation is a perfidious form of fabrication because it involves misusing the truth and using people who trust you.

We see this kind of dishonesty carried to the infinite degree in Judas's "kiss of death." When this faithless disciple betrayed the Lord his signal was, "Whomever I shall kiss, He is the one; seize Him." And immediately he came to Jesus and said, 'Hail, Rabbi;' and kissed Him" (Matt. 26:48,49). It is hard to fathom such brazen boldness.

In the sixth chapter of Proverbs, Solomon painted a word portrait of a manipulator. "A worthless person, a wicked man, is the one who walks with a false mouth, who winks with his eyes, who signals with his feet, who points with his fingers; who with perversity in his heart devises evil continually, who spreads strife" (Prov. 6:12-14).

Not a very pretty picture, is it? What are the characteristics of a manipulator? He lies—"walks with a false mouth." Lying isn't merely something he does, it is his life-style. He is habitually deceitful because "with perversity in his heart [he] devises evil *continually* [and] spreads strife."

A manipulator also uses what psychologists call body language to make inferences and further his cause. He "winks with his eyes" and "signals with his feet," and "points with his fingers." He silently mocks like a child who sticks out his tongue behind the teacher's back.

Ultimately he destroys himself because "his calamity will come suddenly; instantly he will be broken, and there will be no healing" (v. 15). We need to examine our communication patterns and see if we are being candid and aboveboard or if we try to maneuver people.

A seventh form of lying is hypocrisy: saying one thing and being or believing another. A hypocrite is someone whose words and actions don't match. He pretends to be something he is not, sometimes to the point of faking emotions and feelings to cover what lurks under the surface of his soul.

When Christ was indicting the resident hypocrites of His time, the scribes and Pharisees, He described them as people who "honor Me with their lips, but their heart is far away from Me. But in vain do they worship Me, teaching as their doctrines the precepts of men" (Matt. 15:8,9). So a hypocrite has an unfaithful spirit.

Ironically, Solomon, the Spirit-inspired author of Proverbs, was a hypocrite. In his latter years he forsook the teachings of the Lord and brought idol worship into the Temple when he took pagan women as his concubines. He lived in total contradiction to the teachings that the Spirit of God had led him to pen.

He drank to excess: "I explored with my mind how to stimulate my body with wine" (Eccles. 2:3) after writing, "It is not for kings to drink wine" (Prov. 31:4). He sought after material possessions: "I enlarged my works: I built houses for myself . . . bought male and female slaves, . . . possessed flocks and herds larger than all who preceded me in Jerusalem . . . collected for myself silver and gold" (Eccles. 2:4,7,8). This from one who counseled, "Do not weary yourself to gain riches, cease from your consideration of it" (Prov. 23:4).

He practiced sexual immorality: "I provided for myself . . . the pleasures of men—many concubines. . . . All that my eyes desired I did not refuse them. I did not withhold my heart from any pleasure" (Eccles. 2:8,10). This, spoken by the same man who said that those who do not fear the Lord "shall eat of the fruit of their own way, and be satiated with their own devices" (Prov. 1:31).

Solomon betrayed his position and all he believed, and

was miserable because of it. He knew he had been uniquely used and blessed by God because he mused that, "In addition to being a wise man, [I] also taught the people knowledge; and [I] pondered, searched out and arranged many proverbs. [I] sought to find delightful words and to write words of truth correctly" (Eccles. 12:9,10). He was disgusted with what he had become. He was unhappy, depressed and felt guilty. "I hated life, for the work which had been done under the sun was grievous to me; because everything is futility and striving after wind" (Eccles. 2:17).

In the final analysis he determined what all of us must: "The conclusion, when all has been heard, is: fear God and keep His commandments, because this applies to every person. Because God will bring every act to judgment, everything which is hidden, whether it is good or evil" (Eccles. 12:13,14).

Another kind of lying is faithlessness: breaking promises; saying we will do something then not doing it. Now, right at the start, let's clarify what a broken promise is. It is being unfaithful to a commitment when it would be possible to keep it. If I promise to take my son to Disneyland then have an opportunity to go to the ballet so cancel out on him, I have broken trust with him. But if I get the flu, or if my car breaks down, or if emergency expenditures have cut into the budget, then I am not breaking a promise if I postpone the trip. I have no choice but to change our plans.

A promise is a vow, an oath. It involves keeping our word when we say we will do something. A promise carries with it the responsibility to do whatever is necessary to fulfill its stipulations, therefore we must be extremely careful about what we promise and to whom, because verbal commitment is an awesome responsibility.

Remember the promise Peter enthusiastically made to Jesus? "I will *never* fall away. . . . Even if I must die with

You, I will *not* deny You" (Matt. 26:33,35, italics added).

But the Lord knew better. He told Peter that, "This very night, before a cock crows, you shall deny Me three times" (v. 34).

True to Christ's prophecy, Peter was faithless. When a servant girl asked him if he had been with Jesus the Galilean, Peter denied it before a crowd, saying, "I do not know what you are talking about" (v. 70). Then another servant girl saw him and pointed him out and told the people, "This man was with Jesus of Nazareth" (v. 71). But he swore he wasn't. "I do not know the man" (v. 72). Then a little later some of the people who had been standing around came to him and said they knew he was a disciple by the way he talked and he swore at them and yelled, "I do not know the man!" (v. 74). And as soon as he had uttered those words a cock crowed.

The Bible says when this happened Peter remembered what his Lord had told him and he wept bitterly. He had been faithless. I'm sure Peter meant it when he vowed to be true to Jesus. I don't think he thought he would break his promise when he made it. But he lied when he said he would never deny Christ, then later he faced the heartache of knowing he had gone back on his commitment.

Most of us are enough like Peter that we should exercise great discretion when we bind ourselves to a certain course of action. This doesn't apply only to keeping our word but also to our responsibilities to minister. We must be willing to carry through on our Christian commitment to serve.

Results of Lying

Now that we have identified eight kinds of untruths, let's look at the results of lying. It is important that we understand what the aftereffects are, because many people think that when it comes to fabrication the end justifies the means: that it is all right to lie for a valiant or prudent reason.

The first result of lying is that a lie will eventually be uncovered. Proverbs 12:19 says, "Truthful lips will be established forever, but a lying tongue is only for a moment." So we see that lies are transitory but truth endures. God's truth is eternal but falsehoods diminish as quickly as you can wink your eye. Lying never accomplishes anything because when the deception is exposed, the accomplishment is undone.

Let's say I lie to my employer about a colleague so I can get a promotion. What will happen to my position and to my boss's and fellow workers' respect for me, and their estimation of me when that lie is unmasked? And the lie *will* be uncovered because "a lying tongue is only for a moment." Lying is both fruitless and wasteful.

Another result of lying is punishment. "A false witness will not go unpunished, and he who tells lies will not escape" (Prov. 19:5). If we lie we will reap the results of lying and our punishment will come from several sources. Obviously, if we commit perjury in court we are liable under the law and can even spend time in jail. Few if any of us face that danger. But there are other consequences which are just as severe, although they are not imposed by civil law.

When we lie we face *divine punishment*. God will discipline us when we are untruthful. He may expose our lies or He may not; either way we lose. If He does expose us we are discredited. If He does not, we constantly await the moment when He might. Or we suffer because He withholds His blessing from our lives.

When we are exposed we lose credibility so others do not trust us. If people rely on our Christianity and we deal falsely with them in any way, we are no longer believable and neither is the Lord.

Remember the folk tale of the boy who cried wolf? The first few times he gave a false alarm that the wolf was after his flock, people ran to his rescue. And his lie wasn't actually a "bad" one. But he made fools of those who trusted him.

Finally, when he really did need help, no one would listen to his pleas. He had lied so often that when he told the truth no one believed him. That's what happens in human relationships when they are adulterated by lies.

Perhaps the worst punishment we face when we lie is *self-recrimination:* the guilt that results from our sinning, the fear of losing face with friends and loved ones. The knowledge that we got something dishonestly takes all of the pleasure out of what we acquired when we lied. So lack of joy and satisfaction is another by-product of untruthfulness.

Proverbs 20:17 observes that, "Bread obtained by falsehood is sweet to a man, but afterward his mouth will be filled with gravel." Have you ever eaten gravel? Doesn't appeal to your appetite? Not to mine either; but when this proverb was written people would do repentance for verbal sins by eating gravelstones. They would actually chew the pebbles and they would break their teeth and cut their mouths. The stones were not digestible and caused all kinds of physical problems. And, of course the rocks did not satisfy the need for nourishment. Lying is like eating gravel. It ruins pleasure. There is no enduring joy in it; no deep, prolonged sense of satisfaction in a job well done; no clear conscience.

I remember a time when I decided to get some "bread" by falsehood. When I was in college at the University of Kansas there was a football player I wanted to date. He was absolutely gorgeous. All the girls called him "Sexy Rexy." Problem was, one of my best friends, Jan who lived in the same dorm with me, also wanted a date with him.

I heard from one of his fraternity brothers that Sexy Rexy was trying to decide whether to ask Jan or me to a fraternity function. I wanted a date with him so badly I could taste it.

The day he called to ask one of us out, Jan was in Kansas City for the day and I happened to answer the hall phone. He didn't know who I was but I recognized his voice. So when he asked for Jan I said, "Oh, I'm sorry. She's out of town."

Then I added, "And I don't know when she'll be back."
Actually, Kansas City was a 45-minute drive from the university and she was there just for the day.

So Rex said, "Well, could I speak to Jo Gladfelter?"

Now, I knew when he called he'd picked Jan but I didn't mind being second choice. The thought of a date with him seemed so sweet that nothing else mattered. So I went away from the phone for a moment, came back and took the call.

We went on that date and I had the most horrible time I've ever had in my life. All evening I felt guilty. I couldn't carry on a decent conversation. I was afraid he'd mention Jan. Then I started feeling terrible about what I'd done to her. Especially since, when she'd gotten back from Kansas City, the first thing I did was tell her Rex had called and asked me for a date.

Do you know what happened? He called Jan back later and asked her out. He had wanted to go with her anyway. And when they talked he told her how he'd phoned when she was out of town. I almost lost Jan's friendship. I had to face both of them and own up to what I'd done. I learned that "bread obtained by falsehood" may be sweet but it sure turned to gravel for me. Lying *never* works.

Becoming a Truth-Teller

Do you fabricate, in any of the ways we have discussed? If so, you can reverse even minor, untruthful habit patterns if you practice becoming a truth-teller by following some proverbial advice.

Admit that each lie is a sin, not just an indiscretion or an irrelevant fib: that "the mouth of the righteous flows with wisdom, but the perverted tongue will be cut out" (Prov. 10:31).

Practice keeping quiet. Be silent rather than lying. One of the surest ways to keep from lying is to not say anything. "A man of understanding keeps silent" (11:12).

Speak righteously. We may say we lie to keep from hurting others but that is not so. Usually we do it to get what we want. Instead of lying to champion your own cause you should, "Open your mouth for the dumb, for the rights of the unfortunate. Open your mouth, judge righteously, and defend the rights of the afflicted and needy" (31:8,9).

Weigh each word before you say it. Be certain that what you are going to say is the truth, the whole truth and nothing but the truth. "The one who guards his mouth preserves his life; the one who opens wide his lips comes to ruin" (13:3).

Weigh the consequences. Ultimately you will hurt yourself if you lie. Remember, lying is self-destructive, impermanent, brings no satisfaction, kills your joy, and penalizes you with feelings of guilt and fear, plus it destroys trust relationships. "A false witness will not go unpunished, and he who tells lies will perish" (19:9).

Choose to not lie. By an act of the will tell the truth. Ask God to make lying so repulsive to you that you will not do it. "A righteous man hates falsehood; but a wicked man acts disgustingly and shamefully" (13:5).

Confess immediately when you do lie. Expose and conquer. "He who conceals his transgressions will not prosper, but he who confesses and forsakes them will find compassion" (28:13).

Above all, admit that each lie is hated by God, regardless of its size, why you are telling it or how harmless it seems. "The Lord hates . . . a lying tongue" (6:16,17). Make life easier for yourself. Become a truth-teller.

Workshop

1. Some famous proverbs about lies and truth are listed here. Read each one and write your interpretation of it as it applies to you.

    a. When you shoot an arrow of truth, dip its point in honey (Arabian).

b. Speak the truth and run (Yugoslavian).

c. A liar is one who has no partition between his imagination and his information (anon.).

d. A liar has to have a good memory (anon.).

e. The good thing about telling the truth is that you don't have to remember what you said (anon.).

f. Oh, what a tangled web we weave when first we practice to deceive (Sir Walter Scott).

g. It is more from carelessness about truth than from intentional lying that there are so many falsehoods in the world (Samuel Johnson).

2. Match each proverb with what it tells about an honest, truthful person. The first one is done for you.

Proverbs 3:3   tells what is right
Proverbs 10:31   chooses not to lie
Proverbs 12:17   asks God to sustain his truthfulness
Proverbs 12:19   delights the Lord
Proverbs 12:22   clings to the truth
Proverbs 13:5   does not listen to lies
Proverbs 14:5   what he says stands the test of time
Proverbs 21:28   speaks wisely
Proverbs 30:7,8   hates lies and lying

SEVEN

Easier Parenting

A child left to itself disgraces his mother.
Proverbs 29:15 (NIV)

Several months ago, Dear Abby ran a letter in her column from a woman who was heartbroken and disillusioned about motherhood. She told how all of her children had disappointed and hurt her, how each had brought her grief and shame. She said she wished she had never had them and that if she had it to do over again she would remain childless because her children weren't worth the time and effort she had invested in them.

Abby was so shocked by this woman's statements that she decided to poll her readers to see how many of them felt the same way about their offspring. Of the hundreds of thousands who responded, over 80 percent said they agreed with the woman—that they wished their children had *never been born!*

What went wrong? I believe this trend developed because our society has lost its ability to parent. And if our children and our children's children are going to reverse this pattern, it is extremely important that all of us redefine what it means to be a parent and to see what God's Word says about raising children who will be happy, emotionally healthy, productive, godly adults. It is time we stopped bemoaning the difficulties and heartaches of parenthood and started stressing the benefits and looking at what we can do to make it a pleasurable, rewarding experience.

The Parent's Role

As parents, we need to know what our role is for the benefit of our children, to help them, teach them and let them know they can rely on us as they grow toward independence. Instead, too often we focus on what we want our children to do for us: make us proud, bring us pleasure and enjoyment, be a personal asset—a feather in our caps.

When I was in college the instructor of a course on educating the exceptional child, Dr. Sophia Salvin was telling how hard it is for parents of the retarded or handicapped to accept their child's deficiency and she made a statement that stunned my senses. She said this was difficult for them because, "When all is said and done, children are nothing more than an extension of the parents' egos."

At first I bristled. My daughters were preschoolers at the time and the idea that they were tied to my ego was offensive to me. But the more I thought about it the more I realized she was right. I wanted my girls to have good manners, dress fashionably, make good grades and be social butterflies so people would see what a good mother I was; what neat kids I had. I had to learn to want what was best for them rather than what would satisfy my pride.

A good parent views his child as a person, as a feeling, thinking individual, not as a possession.

The parent must be a foundational example. Children learn by what they see, therefore we must be examples to our children of what we want them to become. Why is it, when we think of parenting, we think of what we should *do* rather than what we should *be?* Maybe it is because it's easier to perform ritualistic duties than it is to live godly lives. It is easier to tell someone what to do instead of showing them through consistent example. Proverbs 22:6 says we are to "train up a child in the way he should go, even when he is old he will not depart from it."

We are not commanded to *tell* a child, but *train* him. The child who is instructed mostly with words will easily deviate from what he is told, but one who has been taught by example has his ideals so deeply imbedded into his soul's eye that he will not forsake them, even when he is grown.

The fact that children learn so much by example can be either a detriment or a blessing. I remember a time when a young mother in my Bible class shared that one day she heard her four-year-old daughter playing in her room. The child was alone but she was yelling at someone. So the mother peeked in the door and her daughter was holding her favorite doll by one arm, shaking her and hitting her, shouting, "You bad girl! You stay with me in this store. Do you hear?"

The mother said, "I couldn't believe what I was seeing and hearing. My daughter was imitating me. That's the way I treat her. I have never been so ashamed and humiliated."

Like it or not, every parent is an ongoing example to his child. The issue is not whether we are going to be examples but what kind we will be. Studies show that children of alcoholics have a high rate of alcoholism; people who were abused when they were small also batter their own children. Conversely, children whose parents live righteously produce offspring who do likewise. We should live so as to be able to say to our children, "Give me your heart, my [child] and let your eyes delight in my ways" (Prov. 23:26).

How we live equals the kind of children we will turn out.
If our children are not developing spiritually and morally as
they should, it does not mean there is something wrong with
them but it indicates a lack in our parenting. Dr. Norm
Wakefield says, "As a rule children become what the parents
allow them to become. Usually well-adjusted children are
the products of parents who provide a balanced diet of security, love, friendship, respect and discipline. . . . Faulty children are often the result of faulty parenting."[1]

It is the example we set, not the words we utter, that helps
our children become a blessing to us and to themselves. "A
righteous man who walks in his integrity—how blessed are
his [children] after him" (Prov. 20:7).

Being There for Your Children

Why do some parents fail where others succeed when
outwardly it seems they have done pretty much the same
thing? Is there some mystical, unique combination of characteristics that makes someone a good parent and the few who
are bestowed make it and the others don't? It can't be that our
ability to parent rests on our personalities or our socioecono-
mic status; nor is it contingent on the amount of formal
education we have or our race or religion. I am convinced
that it depends on one thing: being there for our children.

A good parent must be there for his child, as a total
support system, at all times, for "a child left to itself disgraces his mother" (Prov. 29:15, *NIV*). Being there is more
than physical presence. Many parents and children occupy
the same quarters but do not relate to or communicate with
one another. Being there is supplying life-sustaining emotional undergirding and spiritual support, *no matter what*. It
means your child knows he will never have to face life alone,
that you will always share his joy and sorrows, his successes
and failures, his sins and his confessions. It means that a
child knows, regardless of how young or old he is or what he

does, that his parent will never desert him or give up on him.

I will be honest. I am appalled at the number of parents I know who "wash their hands" of their children. They kick them out of the family, they withhold love, they disown them, they turn their backs on them. When my children were born, I inherited the obligation and the privilege of being their mother *until the day I die*. Parenthood, like marriage, is "till death do us part."

But what if your daughter is living with her boyfriend? Aren't there exceptions for the Christian parent? It doesn't matter. She is still your child and you are to be there. Or, what if your son is a junkie? It doesn't matter. He is still your son and you are to be there. What if your 16-year-old daughter drops out of school. It doesn't matter. She is still your child and you are to be there. What if your son was involved in a hit-and-run accident when he was drinking? It doesn't matter. He is still your son and you are to be there. How else can you guide, direct, help?

God, our heavenly Father, never leaves us. Christ promised, "I will not leave you as orphans" (John 14:18)—without parental direction; abandoned and helpless. If we are to exemplify Him in our lives we can never emotionally desert our children.

A classic example of many parents is vividly portrayed in a deodorant commercial on television. A little girl comes into the kitchen, in tears, carrying a broken doll. Her mommy is standing at the stove stirring a pot of something. The little girl tugs on her mother's skirt and shows her the doll. The mother pats her daughter on the head and keeps stirring the pot.

Then the phone rings so the mother stops patting the child on the head, keeps stirring the pot and answers the phone. The little girl is still standing there crying.

Next the doorbell rings and the mother stops stirring the pot, keeps talking on the phone and opens her back door; and the little girl is *still* standing there crying. Then we are told that it is at times like these we need Brand X deodorant.

The message is clear. A child needed comforting but the mother was more concerned with what she was doing. She was not being there for her little girl.

Being there doesn't apply only in times of trouble. You must instill in your child the knowledge that you will help meet his needs at any given moment—in times of rejoicing as well as in times of need; you must convey to him that you are conscious of him and concerned for his well-being even when you are not in his presence.

Right now in Los Angeles we are having the heaviest rains we've had in years. Both of our daughters have their own apartments; one has to drive a canyon road which the radio warned is flooded out, and the other the San Diego Freeway which is also deluged today. So I was praying for them this morning during the time I knew they would be on the road on their way to work.

About 8:15 the phone rang. It was Brenda, our 24-year-old, and I expected her to tell me her car had broken down, which it has an expensive habit of doing. Instead, she said, "I just called to let you know I didn't go to work today. The road is just too bad and the street by my office is closed. I knew you'd be praying and figured I'd let you know you had one less of us to worry about." She knew I would be worried about her and be praying for her—that I would be there. That's what parents are for.

What It Means to Be There

Being there means we direct and disciple our children. We do not leave them to their own devices. Proverbs 1:2-4 lists seven things we are to instruct to them. We are (1) to teach them to "know wisdom"—how to properly use knowledge; (2) to "discern the sayings of understanding"— think matters through to an intelligent conclusion; (3) to "receive instruction in wise behavior"—show them how to act as God would have them act; (4) to teach them about "righteousness, justice and equity"—what is right, fair, moral; (5) to give "prudence to the naive"—help them develop the ability to detect deceit; (6) to see that they receive proper "knowledge"—that the right facts and values are programmed into their souls; and (7) to teach "discretion"—the ability to judge what is proper and correct.

A major ingredient in directing and discipling is *discipline*—which doesn't necessarily mean punishing. And a major ingredient of discipline on your part is consistency. Inconsistency is the most difficult thing in the world to live with because you have no boundaries for your behavior, no point of reference. If a child does the same thing twice and gets a favorable reaction one time and a negative one the next, how does he decide which behavior pattern is acceptable and which is not?

Consistency doesn't mean having a lot of rules—just strictly adhering to the ones you feel are important to your child's welfare, and responding in an unchanging, constant manner to his behavior. Jay Kesler, president of Youth for Christ International, also believes these rules should serve a purpose beyond just forcing the child to act in a certain way. He says, "The rules and disciplines of our households should not be aimed at simply keeping control and order. There is more to it all. Rules are teaching tools."[2]

If we establish rules and penalties for infringing on those rules, then neglect to carry through with the penalty, we defeat the entire purpose of making guidelines. If we are inconsistent we worry our children. If we don't do what we said we were going to do we create anxiety because, "Hope deferred makes the heart sick, but desire fulfilled is a tree of life" (Prov. 13:12). That is true even when it pertains to punishment. If you tell a child you will spank him if he does something and one time you carry through and the next time you don't, your child will be confused and will do everything within his power to try to persuade you to let him operate on the exception rather than the rule.

We need to understand why we tend to be so inconsistent. One reason is because we think we are doing our children a favor by backing off, by postponing punishment; but we are not, because "He who spares his rod hates his son, but he who loves him disciplines him diligently" (Prov. 13:24).

Another reason for our inconsistency is that our responses depend on our reaction at any given moment rather than on an established, fair manner of discipline. The child disobeys. We get angry. *Our* comfort has been disturbed. *Our* pride is hurt. *Our* possessions are ruined. *Our* time infringed upon. So we retaliate emotionally rather than doing what would be most beneficial for the child.

Consistency is especially important for very young children. For example, at our house lying is always punishable. When the children were small a lie equaled an automatic spanking. When they were older it meant grounding for a week. No exceptions, because George and I both believe children must be taught to tell their parents the truth.

We also had established that missing curfew meant automatic grounding. There were times when one of the girls came home late for a good reason—which we could believe because our kids knew what we would do if we caught them lying—so we let her off the hook. Generally, a rule made is a rule to be obeyed. We have to have enough confidence in ourselves as parents to be consistent in what we expect and to carry through on disciplinary measures.

Being there means we help our children develop values. We must teach them how to select the right kind of friends because, "He who walks with wise men will be wise, but the companion of fools will suffer harm" (Prov. 13:20). We should stress the benefit of a good reputation, for, "a good name is to be more desired than great riches" (22:1).

We are committed to instilling God's moral standards into their natures, "—to deliver [them] from the way of evil" (2:12). We must help them set and strive toward goals, because without direction and discipline they will not become fulfilled. "He who follows empty pursuits will have poverty in plenty" (28:19). We should let them know we have high expectations for them; that what they do affects our well-being as well as their own.

Our children need to know that they can bring great joy into our lives and that a large portion of our happiness is contingent on their being happy too. Solomon summarized his parental expectations to his son this way: "My son, if your heart is wise, my own heart also will be glad; and my inmost being will rejoice, when your lips speak what is right" (23:15,16).

Being there means we understand our children's needs and do everything within our human power to meet those needs. Three of those needs are: love, encouragement and understanding. How, according to King Solomon, can we love, encourage and understand our children?

Love is every child's primary need. Solomon indicated it is to be an unqualified love that "covers all transgressions" (10:12). Just as God's love for us is unconditional, so must our love for our children be. We must accept them just as they are, allowing for flaws and not letting their human deficiencies become barriers in the relationship. No child should have to "win" his parents' affection.

Saying "I love you" is important, but not sufficient. The love relationship between parent and child must involve *intimacy*. It is hugging, kissing—physical contact. It is secret telling—sharing together things you share with no one else. It is a smile that says, "I like you." Your child should know that if he wasn't part of your life you would be less than complete because he is the only person in the world who can touch certain areas of your heart.

We destroy intimacy when we make the child's performance, rather than his presence, the basis for our love. When
we care more about how he acts than who he is or make his
behavior rather than his person the vital factor in our relationship we block any chance for closeness.

Involvement is also a component of parental love. If we
isolate or set ourselves apart we stop being parents and
become parent figures. Some parents operate on the "let
someone else do it" theory. Let someone else be the basket-
ball coach, the scout leader, or drive the kids to the zoo, be
room mother, have the slumber party at their house. Partici-
pating in everyday events that are important to your child
shows him you love him.

Parents must get involved in their children's problems.
Many parents run from the reality of their children's problems instead of attacking and solving them. I think that is
because they don't want to face their own failure. But running only compounds the situation. Children and young
people are not capable of handling life's difficulties alone.
That is why they have parents. *Your child's problems are
things you go through with him!*

Another need children have is big, daily doses of encouragement. Growing up is hard. They need parents who
will spur them on when they get discouraged because "no one
can bear a broken spirit" (see Prov. 18:14). They need to be
told they are capable, shown what their talents are and how to
develop their special abilities, taught that defeat isn't bad and
that winning isn't everything; that trying is what counts.

Children are different from adults. They don't know
what we know or reason the way we reason. They are
immature. They are childish and they need understanding.
They do not need our expectations imposed on them. The
better we understand our children the more pleasurable our
relationship with them will be because "good understanding
produces favor" (Prov. 13:15).

We as parents must be sensitive to what our children do not know and what they cannot do or we will expect too much from them for their age, size and maturity. We must perceive what hurts their feelings so we will not wound them emotionally. Dr. Norm Wakefield has observed that "many well-meaning adults fail to sense disappointment, frustration, loneliness, and a host of other feelings in the child. They cannot read the signals that their youngsters send."[3]

We need to watch our children's reactions so we can discern their true feelings. Children experience great frustration at their inability to verbally communicate how they feel, so we have to read their actions. That is why young children frequently will lash out at a parent saying they "hate" him. The child may be angry, resentful, jealous, feel slighted or be frustrated because he can't tie his shoes, but he cannot express those emotions in words so he blurts, "I hate you!"

Instead of reacting to such a "terrible statement" like a wounded adult because our pride has been hurt, we need to be understanding and help the child sort through how he actually feels and why. An appropriate response to this kind of outburst would be, "I can tell you are very angry. Can you tell me why?" When we help our children talk about their feelings they learn to define and handle their emotions.

Being there means that we can be tools to hone our children into what they should be. "Iron sharpens iron, so one man sharpens another" (Prov. 27:17). This sharpening to maturity occurs when we as parents form in a child that essential we call self-image. This most crucial, lasting part of the child's self-concept is programmed into him before he is old enough to have any control over it. He is totally at the mercy of his environment during those first tender formative years of his life. And more than anyone else he looks to his parents to show him who he is. So we must discover what it is God wants us to show each of our children about himself or herself, because a child's entire life is affected by the conclusions he draws from our reactions and observations.

A young child has no way of distinguishing whether our assessment of him is accurate or erroneous. If we relay faulty concepts, the child will believe they are true. If we state untruths or exaggerate or say something we do not mean out of anger, our child does not know that.

We can help our children develop a proper sense of self-esteem if we label their actions instead of attacking the children personally. Unwarrranted value judgments destroy the personhood of our child. Honest judgments, where we show him both his strengths and shortcomings, build the child's character. Attacking him means we judge, shame and belittle him by issuing verdicts about what he is like. Labeling actions means we state a fact and offer positive input.

For instance, saying, "You are so slow that we are always late no matter where we go," is an attack on the child. It is an exaggerated verdict. No child can always make someone late. "We were late because you didn't get ready on time. Next time you need to start getting ready earlier," is labeling his actions and offering a solution. Attack his problem, not his person!

Maintaining a Child's Dignity

Children need to be treated as caring, feeling, thinking human beings; to be approached with dignity and concern. Too often we speak to and treat them as "lesser" than adults just because they are smaller and younger. This is prejudice of the worst kind.

The disciples displayed such an attitude toward some little ones who wanted to touch the Lord. They "rebuked [the children]. But when Jesus saw this, He was indignant and said to them, 'Permit the children to come to Me; do not hinder them; for the kingdom of God belongs to such as these' " (Mark 10:13,14). Jesus loved children because they were children, and so should we.

How can you maintain a child's dignity and still not sacrifice your parental respect and authority?

You maintain a child's dignity by never putting him down. You must do what will help, not defeat him; edify, not degrade. You must be more concerned about what will happen to the child than about what other people will think about the way he behaves. You must respect his prerogative to be a person in his own right and not just an extension of his parents, teachers and associates.

You maintain a child's dignity by treating him with respect and courtesy. I will always remember a time when I was teaching school and had a student teacher assigned to me for a semester. I was observing a lesson she was teaching about manners and the rules of courtesy. She did an outstanding job, showing the kids how to greet people, say excuse me, reply respectfully to others and help seat adults. Then, at the end of the lesson, as she was walking over to her desk, she accidentally stepped on a little boy's toe. She turned to him and snapped, "Get your feet out of the way."

She reacted to the child the way a lot of adults would. Have you ever noticed how we demand that children say please and thank you and excuse themselves when they walk in front of us or interrupt us but how seldom we return the favor? Often we are plain rude to children, talking to them in tones we would never use to an adult; displaying bad manners toward them. Children deserve to be treated with respect.

You maintain a child's dignity by offering him choices; by giving him a way to save face and still comply with your wishes. You can do this even with very young children. For example, if your toddler is misbehaving at the table and won't stop, the choices might be: (1) finish your dinner and then you can eat some dessert; (2) get down; (3) have Mommy give you a spanking and go to your room until the rest of us finish eating.

Offering choices is particularly important during the teens. Children who are bordering adulthood need to make decisions and decide between various opportunities. They resent being backed into a corner with ultimatums and need to be presented with alternatives; to be offered workable solutions. We need to remember that God tempers His justice with mercy, His power with love. So should we for our children.

Sometimes we back ourselves into a corner by making unreasonable demands or imposing too harsh a punishment, then we won't back down because of our pride. We need to be fair more than we need to be right because, "The execution of justice is joy for the righteous, but is terror to the workers of iniquity" (Prov. 21:15). There is no place for hardheadedness or hard-heartedness in the parent-child relationship because, "He who hardens his heart will fall into calamity" (28:14).

You also maintain a child's dignity by offering explanations for what you do, for the disciplines you impose and the standards of conduct you require. For some reason adults think if they explain why they are doing something they will lose their child's respect. Actually, the opposite is true. Offering reasons does not detract from your authority but reinforces it; it builds understanding and helps a child see what your motives are. If you make a demand of your child, he has a right to know why.

Nothing upsets me more than to hear a father or mother say, "You have to do this just because I said to." That's a dignity detractor. It's the same as telling a child he is not important enough to give answers to. Proverbs 22:15 declares that, "Foolishness is bound up in the heart of a child," but to the child, his ideas, his conclusions and his actions don't seem foolish at all. They make perfect sense to his immature mind. How will he learn what is foolish and what is wise if you don't explain it to him?

Our relationships with our children will improve as we offer explanations and answer their questions because "a man has joy in an apt answer, and how delightful is a timely word!" (15:23).

Lastly, you maintain a child's dignity by never embarrassing him. If you make fun of a child or reprimand him in front of others, especially his peers, you are not punishing him, you are demoralizing him. None of us likes to be called down in public; to have someone get onto us in front of our friends.

There is a difference between a parent embarrassing a child and the child's behavior being an embarrassment in itself. If a child misbehaves or if a teenager is rude in front of his buddies and loses face because of it, he has embarrassed himself. We, as parents, must take care not to do anything to make our children look bad to others. We want to help them put their best foot forward, not accentuate their faults.

Be Honest with Your Child

Parents should be as open and honest with their children as they can be. I am not intimating that we purposely lie, but we do not disclose ourselves fully to them. We hide our feelings and, in doing so, teach them to hide theirs.

For instance, let's say you've had a frustrating day. A package you were expecting in the mail didn't come, the car broke down, and the dog dug up your neighbor's garden. Your second-grader comes bouncing in the house after school and you reply to his cheery greeting with a mumbled hello. He knows by the tone of your voice something is bothering you so he asks what's wrong. You tell him, "Nothing."

Now he *knows* something is wrong and immediately fears it relates to him so asks, "Are you mad at me?" To which you snap, "No. Now just leave me alone."

So he goes to his room, confused and frightened,

wondering what's the matter, and the entire scene could have been eliminated if you had given an honest answer. You could have told him you had a lousy day and are in a grumpy mood.

Rather than disillusioning our children, a frank admission of feelings or a simple statement about a situation—even if it is unpleasant—will keep open the lines of communication. Children know when we are withholding but they cannot evaluate our motives because we are not open with them. When we admit and deal with our emotions or problems our children learn how to deal with theirs.

Instead of admitting problems we teach our children to cover up. What's the first thing we say to a child when he falls down and hurts himself? "Don't cry," which translated means, "Don't show how you feel." We do this when there is friction in the family. We tell them Mom and Dad didn't have a fight when the child heard us through the walls the night before. Or, we tell them they don't need to buy something when what we really mean is that we can't afford it.

Dr. James Dobson says, "Though it is hard to accept at the time, our child also needs the minor setbacks and disappointments which come his way. . . . Our task as parents, then, is not to eliminate every challenge for our children; it is to serve as a confident ally on their behalf, . . . above all, giving them the tools with which to overcome obstacles."[4]

We don't have to recite details or dump more on a child than he can handle, but we do need to share our problems. Proverbs 11:1 notes, "A false balance is an abomination to the Lord." We, as caring parents, should present a balanced picture to our children, involving them in the good and bad times, the happiness and grief, the pleasures and problems by being honest with them about our life situation.

In conclusion, Solomon observed that, "A cheerful heart has a continual feast" (Prov. 15:15). Children must be allowed to be children, to have fun, to participate in activities they enjoy. We need to create an environment where kids can be kids; where they can relax, spill things, work and play without stress, listen to music, have space of their own and express themselves emotionally, creatively and intellectually: where they can have fun.

Let's not leave our children to themselves or be remote dictators but accept the full realm of parenthood by being there and doing all that is within our power to meet their needs, remembering that, "A child left to itself disgraces his mother" (29:15, *NIV*), but "a wise son makes his parents glad" (see Prov. 10:1).

Workshop

1. Look up each proverb then list the principle in it that should be taught to a child.

Reference	Principle
3:11	
3:31	
4:1-4	
4:10	
5:1-7	
7:1,2	
7:24	

Now summarize the overall idea in these sayings, in your own words.

2. Look up the following Scriptures and list what we as parents are supposed to teach to our children.

Reference	Lesson
2:2-5	
3:3	
4:7-9	
4:13	
5:8-14	
6:23	
7:24-27	

3. Look up each Scripture then list what it says about our approach to our children.

Reference	Approach
13:24	
17:25	
22:15	
19:18,27	
22:6	
23:13,14	
23:24	

4. Some famous non-biblical proverbs about children are listed here. Read each one and write your interpretation of it, as it applies to you.

    a. Happy is the man who is taught his folly in his youth (anon.).

    b. Love lives in cottages as well as courts (English).

    c. They do not love that do not show their love (John Heywood).

    d. It is a wise father that knows his own child (Shakespeare).

    e. A burnt child dreads the fire (anon.).

    f. Correction is good only if administered in time (anon.).

g. He that has learned to obey will know how to command (Solon).

h. A child's education should begin at least one hundred years before he is born (Oliver Wendell Holmes).

i. Being a good parent means you know when to hug, when to holler and when to hogtie (anon.).

j. Youth supposes, age knows (Welsh).

Notes

1. Norm Wakefield, *You Can Have a Happier Family* (Ventura, CA: Regal Books, 1977), p. 12.
2. Jay Kesler, *Too Big to Spank* (Ventura, CA: Regal Books, 1978), p. 64.
3. Wakefield, p. 68.
4. James Dobson, *Hide or Seek* (Old Tappan, NJ: Fleming H. Revell, 1974), p. 70.

EIGHT

Pride vs. Humility

When pride comes, then comes dishonor,
but with the humble is wisdom.
Proverbs 11:2

It was just a little bush. It had probably taken root from a seed that had blown into the yard. I was amazed as I watched it grow to full bloom during the next few weeks. It was massive—at least five feet high and it spanned a width of four feet in front of the planter. In the fall, when it died out, black pods about the size of peas dropped onto the ground from inside the magenta flowers. By the time winter arrived, the bush had disappeared except for a shriveled inch-high stub.

When winter turned into spring, instead of one alien bush sprouting, dozens of them poked their heads from beneath the sod. The entire planter was overrun with magenta-flowered bushes. I tried to dig out each plant, but despite my efforts several persisted and by the following year they had developed such an intricate root system that they wrapped around the mock-orange bush, almost killing it. They choked out the ground cover.

Finally, to rid ourselves of those unwelcome pests, we had to dig up the entire planter in front of our house. When we did we found that the roots not only intertwined but went several feet deep, forming an almost impenetrable network.

It was three years ago this spring that we dug up those pretty, but pesky, bushes. Yesterday, as I was pulling weeds in the planter I noticed that in the spot where the original bush had been a plant was pushing through the soil, persistently splitting the earth and rearing its unwanted head. Somehow, when we dug up the planter we must have missed some of the roots. And the cycle will start over again unless we immediately destroy that bush which is the source of a growth we do not want in our yard. Somehow, we will have to kill its roots or it will again overtake the other plants.

The Origin of Pride

God's Word teaches that pride is like that plant: a sin that is deeply imbedded in our soul, intrinsic to our nature, one that gives birth to many other kinds of sins; that rears its ugly head when we are certain we have extracted it. And unless we recognize it for what it is, we will fall victim to it and be encumbered by it and rendered ineffective because, "When pride comes, then comes dishonor" (Prov. 11:2).

Any plant needs roots to grow. Cut out its roots and it will die. Evil also needs roots—an unholy source that will keep it alive: and that root in the lives of God's righteous is the sin of pride. Pride is a *root sin!*

Just as the roots of a plant push deeply into the soil and supply essential nourishment, pride wedges itself into our character and nurtures our sense of self-importance, feeding the big "I." It gives growth and is the basis of all other sins. So if we can eliminate the sin of pride our other iniquities will subside and our lives will be easier.

Yes, pride is a root sin. It caused Satan, the angel whom God had created to be the special protector of the very throne of heaven, who had the "seal of perfection, [and was] full of wisdom and perfect in beauty" (Ezek. 28:12) to want even more. He wanted to be like God: to usurp God's position and power, to be raised above the Lord in stature, to secure for himself the praise, adoration and worship God alone deserves. He proclaimed, "I will make myself like the Most High" (Isa. 14:14).

Why, when he had so much, did Satan seek greater things? Scripture says it was because of his conceit. The Lord rebuked him for it, saying, "Your heart was lifted up because of your beauty; you corrupted your wisdom by reason of your splendor" (Ezek. 28:17). Satan became prideful because of what God had done for him. He wasn't responsible for his wisdom or beauty nor the position to which he had been assigned. God created him and appointed him to his designated task. It is easy to see how the self-centered nature of the sin of pride alienates us from God.

The Lord reminds us in Proverbs that our destiny is in His hands; that who and what we become is of His choosing, not ours, and that any accolades belong to Him, not to us. He urges us to keep our perspective. "The hearing ear and the seeing eye, the Lord has made both of them. . . . The rich and the poor have a common bond, the Lord is the maker of them all. . . . The poor man and the oppressor have this in common: the Lord gives light to the eyes of both" (Prov. 20:12; 22:2; 29:13).

He also cautions that "if you have been foolish in exalting yourself . . . put your hand on your mouth" (30:32). He warns us to kill the roots of pride! "Let another praise you, and not your own mouth; a stranger, and not your own lips" (27:2).

The same root sin of pride that motivated Satan caused man's fall. Eve succumbed to temptation when Satan, disguised as the beguiling serpent, promised her, "*YOU* will be like God"! (Gen. 3:5). So she saw, took and ate of the forbidden fruit because she wanted to be like the Most High; which is the identical reason Satan fell from grace. If pride was the root for the downfall of mankind, it seems logical to assume it is also the foundational element for other sins.

W.B. Eerdmans, a great theologian and expositor of the Scriptures, believed that, "Pride is at the bottom of all didobedience and rebellion against God's laws."[1] So because we are rooted in pride (even those of us who belong to God and are charged by both the words and example of the Lord Jesus Christ to be humble) we readily fall prey to our positions and accomplishments and become people-pleasers and self-exalters.

The Nature of Pride

Pride has many distinguishing attributes.

It is the nature of pride to be self-promoting—to seek glory for itself. Because we have this tendency, God tells us that, "It is . . . not glory to search out one's own glory" (Prov. 25:27). Honor we bestow on ourselves or distinctions we contrive are not true veneration. And our efforts at self-exaltation will fail because, "The Lord will tear down the house of the proud" (15:25).

It is also the nature of pride to debase and devalue the rights and opinions of others. Pride convinces us that we know it all, that we and we alone have the correct answers; that we deserve respect, that we are "better" than those around us, therefore they should admire and follow us.

This, according to Proverbs, is arrogance of the highest degree. "There is a kind who is pure in his own eyes, yet is not washed from his filthiness. There is a kind—oh how lofty are his eyes! And his eyelids are raised in arrogance" (30:12,13). And when our eyelids are raised we look down on others.

This kind of pomposity not only alienates the admiration we seek but it is dangerous. For our own welfare, we should avoid it because "pride goes before destruction, and a haughty spirit before stumbling" (16:18). My daddy used to say that if your nose is too high in the air you're apt to trip over your feet. High-mindedness is self-destructive because it will eventually bring us low.

It is the nature of pride to think it possesses a superior intellect. Pride bloats our ego; it makes us wise in our own eyes. It convinces us that we have arrived spiritually, that *our* way is *the* way, *the* truth, *the* light. We play God and, in many instances, pridefully usurp the duties assigned to the Holy Spirit.

The pseudo-spiritual wisdom which pride generates makes us try to possess and control what people think and do—a task that belongs solely to the Lord of the universe. We decide how others, including our Christian brothers and sisters, should live their lives, what their spiritual obligations and their religious beliefs should be, what doctrinal stands they should take, where they should attend church, with whom they should associate and how spiritually mature they are. We impose our interpretations of Scripture and our views on them in the name of love. No wonder we are told that, "Haughty eyes and a proud heart . . . is sin. . . . The fear of the Lord is to hate evil; pride and arrogance and the evil way" (21:4: 8:13).

Solomon, whom the Bible says was the wisest man who ever lived, equated the person who is wise in his own eyes with a fool—a senseless egotist who, as David put it, "has said in his heart 'There is no God' " (Ps. 53:1). Solomon said, "Do you see a man wise in his own eyes? There is more hope for a fool than for him" (Prov. 26:12). It is ridiculous to think we are spiritually sufficient in any way. God is our only sufficiency.

Finally, it is the nature of pride to give impetus to many other sins. Hatred stems from pride because vanity makes us detest and have contempt for anything or anyone who detracts from our importance. *Selfishness* is another fruit of pride. It causes us to think only of ourselves and disregard the feelings and needs of others. We dwell on what we want and are getting rather than what we can give.

Another ego "flower" that stems from the root sin of pride is *stubbornness*. Pride demands its own way and will not compromise or listen to reason. *Greed* is based in pride; conceit makes us seek what will comfort and edify self, to take positions and acquire possessions that will make us look important.

Jealousy and *envy,* wanting to be what someone else is or to have what they have, are by-products of arrogance. So is *anger,* because egotism makes us resist anything or anyone who gets in our way, who disagrees with us or steals any portion of our glory. There is no doubt about it, pride is at the base of our transgressions.

God hates pride. "A proud look" heads the list of the seven sins that are an abomination to Him (see Prov. 6:16). There are several reasons why He so passionately abhors vanity. It is a cold, cruel, ugly thing that detracts from our witness and stifles love. It belittles our righteousness and compels us to judge others rather than being compassionate and understanding.

God detests pride because it breeds dishonesty and He is truth. It turns us into phonies who nurture exaggerated opinions of ourselves.

Mainly, God cannot and will not honor or tolerate pride because it sets us against Him, causing us to seek our will, not His; our way instead of the path of righteousness. Not only does He hate it, he retaliates against it and chastises anyone who is high-minded. "Everyone who is proud in heart is an abomination to the Lord; assuredly, he will not be unpunished" (16:5).

The Symptoms of Pride

The reason our vanity is able to get such a strong foothold in our souls and create problems for us is that it is not easily recognized. Pride is blind to itself. We are able to see it in others but we do not notice it in ourselves. We cannot see our sin so we are trapped by it. "All the ways of a man are clean in his own sight. . . . There is a way which seems right to a man, but its end is the way of death. . . . His own iniquities will capture the wicked, and he will be held with the cords of his sin" (16:2,25; 5:22).

It is only with God's help, through the conviction of His Spirit and the truth in His Word, that we can discern this shortcoming. The Proverbs help us isolate and identify the sin of pride by describing some of its basic symptoms. Three of its symptoms are named in 21:24: " 'Proud,' 'Haughty,' 'Scoffer,' are his names, who acts with insolent pride." When we discover how it manifests itself we can find ways to eliminate it.

The first symptom of pride in this verse, "Proud," actually means presumptuous in the original Hebrew language. An egotistical person presumes on others. He assumes he knows what they want to do or how they think. He has a know-it-all attitude and is inconsiderate and rude.

A second symptom mentioned here is haughtiness. In our modern vernacular a haughty person would be called a snob or a phony. He is someone who thinks he is better than others, who is status conscious, aloof, patronizing and a name-dropper.

A scoffer is someone who makes fun of people and ideas that do not coincide with his values and opinions. He derides and ridicules anyone who does not live up to his personal standards and expectations.

All of these are symptoms of "insolent pride," which is an immoderate smugness. An insolent person is angered at any intrusion on self and is certain he always knows best. He believes there are only two ways to think or act—the wrong way or his way.

Proverbs 25:14 gives us another symptom of pride— boasting. "Like clouds and wind without rain is a man who boasts of his gifts falsely." Boasting is telling everyone how great you are. In today's society this kind of person is known as a "windbag" or is said to be "full of hot air."

A person who boasts is like a fluffy, airy cloud—he has no substance and serves no purpose. While bragging about our legitimate talents and accomplishments is less than modest, false boasting is even worse. It is exalting what we aren't: being pretentious and supercilious and looking down our noses at those we consider inferior.

Another symptom of pride is self-glorification or self-promotion. Proverbs 25:27 notes that, "It is not good to eat much honey, nor is it glory to search out one's own glory." What does this interesting parallel mean? It implies that eating too much honey can be detrimental to our physical health. It can upset our blood sugar level, thereby affecting our thinking processes. It adds weight and can create an addiction to sweets to the point where we crave it and hurt when we do without it.

Glory-seeking is like eating too much honey. Basically, it also is detrimental to our well-being. Self-promotion makes us high-minded, affects our opinion of ourselves and generates a craving for more acclaim to the point where we hurt when we do without it or have to share the limelight with someone else. We become addicted to the attention we receive. Soon we get so self-centered that we lose sight of the greatness of God. Our mental and spiritual health suffers. Ultimately, self-glorification is self-defeating.

Are you suffering from any of the symptoms we discussed? Do you exalt yourself at the expense of others, have a know-it-all attitude, mock people who disagree with you, or get angry when you are criticized or challenged? Are you presumptuous or snobbish? Immodest or a braggart? Do you boast falsely to draw attention to yourself, and search for settings and situations that make you look good? Do you promote yourself and your causes and possibly have a "superiority" complex?

Remember, we found that pride is blind to itself. It doesn't come packaged the way we expect but it creeps out in subtle ways. It may appear in the form of "false humility," where we take pride in the fact that we aren't proud. Telling someone how awful or unworthy we are attracts just as much attention as telling them how wonderful we are. If we are pleased that we aren't proud, we had better take a closer look.

As we look for pride problems, we must in all sincerity ask God to reveal them to us. And we dare not think we are ever rid of our arrogance, our loftiness, our inflated sense of self. We never will be, and we must constantly prune our pride to stunt its growth.

The Results of Pride

Does pride accomplish what we want it to? Does it bring us respect, honor and esteem? On the contrary, the Bible teaches that, "When pride comes, then comes dishonor. . . . The Lord will tear down the house of the proud. . . . Before destruction the heart of man is haughty. . . . A man's pride will bring him low but a humble spirit will obtain honor" (Prov. 11:2; 15:25; 18:12; 29:23).

I don't believe any of us want that kind of tribulation. We want to be appreciated and accepted but boasting and self-promotion do not generate those positives. Instead, pride gives birth to the things we dread most: dishonor, failure, debasement and destruction!

Pride induces failure because it causes us to take on more than we can handle or to set unrealistic goals, so we stumble. Pride won't let us admit when we are wrong or seek advice, so we don't grow or improve. Instead, we regress—we are brought low.

Pride brings dishonor while demanding honor. It dreads shame and disgrace. That is why prideful people cannot stand criticism. It wounds their egos. Disagreement detracts from the confirmation they require.

Pride generates a pseudo self-confidence that peaks prior to destruction. God will use our pride to tear us down and force us to see the devastating effects of conceit in our lives and upon others. The prouder we become the more danger we face. An anonymous old proverb notes, "Never stand on your pride. If you do, you will surely slip and fall."

How can we avoid such calamity? God's Word says that the antidote for this poisonous root sin is a commodity called humility. In Psalm 131:1, David defined this unique attribute. He sang, "O Lord, my heart is not proud, or my eyes haughty; nor do I involve myself in great matters, or in things too difficult for me."

So a person who is truly humble recognizes both his capabilities and his limitations. He does not become involved in "great matters"—work his way into places where he does not belong or into situations he is not capable of handling. Neither does he get in over his head, pridefully overextending himself where he is not trained, educated or talented. He does not "think more highly of himself than he ought to think; but [he has] . . . sound judgment, as God has allotted to each a measure of faith" (Rom. 12:3). He knows both his strength and weaknesses, and is neither immodest nor deprecatory about himself.

Whereas pride stresses self-excellence, humility is gentle, meek, unassuming and subservient, and "with the humble is wisdom" (Prov. 11:2). C. I. Scofield points out the presence of Christ in the book of Proverbs. He determined that, "In Proverbs wisdom is more than the personification of a divine attribute; it is a foreshadowing of Christ. If you will read 'Christ' instead of 'wisdom' in the passages where the latter word occurs, you will see the supernatural power of this book."[2]

So when we read in Proverbs 11:2: "When pride comes, then comes dishonor, but with the humble is wisdom," we can surmise that Christ, the personification of God's wisdom, is with the wise. He is the epitome of humility, "who although He existed in the form of God, did not regard equality with God a thing to be grasped, but emptied Himself, taking the form of a bondservant, and being made in the likeness of men. And being found in appearance as a man, He *humbled Himself* by becoming obedient to the point of death, even death on a cross" (Phil. 2:6-8, italics added).

The evident solution to pride lies in our willingness to humble ourselves and to be obedient to a loving God who hates arrogance. To do this, we must go against the very fiber of our being, resisting a deeply ingrown trait. But the results are worth it.

Results of Humility

One of the prime results of humility is honor. "Before honor comes humility. . . . Humility goes before honor. . . . A humble spirit will obtain honor" (Prov. 15:33; 18:12; 29:23). How amazing! Humility brings us the honor we crave. What pride requires, humility dispenses.

It seems like a quirk in the structure of things that pride—where we strive to be exalted—is debasing, and humility—where we purposely take the lowly position—is exalting; but that is how God has structured it. Actually it isn't difficult to understand why this happens. To be honored means to be highly regarded and respected. Humility brings this kind of recognition because a humble person sees his imperfections and tries to eliminate them. He praises others rather than himself and as he lauds them they, in response, commend him. He is honored because of his humility.

Humility also embodies certain material and emotional blessings. "The reward of humility and the fear of the Lord are riches, honor and life" (22:4). Notice that humility and reverence of the Lord go hand in hand. A humble person exalts God, who in turn exalts the meek.

Just as pride is punished, humility is rewarded in several ways.

First, humility is rewarded with riches. The wealth may be tangible—physical possessions and money, but it is also the spiritual bounties which God bestows on those who obediently forsake their pride. "It is the blessing of the Lord that makes rich, and he adds no sorrow to it" (10:22).

Humility is also recompensed with honor, which we have already discussed, and with life. That may mean we live longer referring to the quantity of life, but it also alludes to a superior quality of existence, including the abundance Christ promises when we place our trust in Him. Life also refers to the eternal life the Lord grants those who come to Him in faith.

Another outgrowth of humility is improved interpersonal relationships. One way a prideful person draws attention to himself is by associating with people who have recognition and position. This feeds his ego. But the Proverbs tell us that, "It is better to be of a humble spirit with the lowly, than to divide the spoil with the proud" (16:19).

It appears that both pride and humility are "contagious." Being with people who are modest and unpretentious exerts a positive influence on us and keeps us humble. When we have a humble spirit we are easier to get along with; less demanding, more submissive. As we build others up, interpersonal relationships improve.

Humility makes us face our unworthiness and the immensity of God's grace. It brings us closer to God, "For though the Lord is exalted, yet He regards the lowly" (Ps. 138:6).

It equips us to love. Pride negates love. Love "is not jealous; . . . does not brag and is not arrogant, does not act unbecomingly; it does not seek its own, is not provoked, does not take into account a wrong suffered" (1 Cor. 13:4,5). Love, therefore, is humble. Conversely, when we are humble we are loving.

A final result of humility is honest praise. If what we do is truly noteworthy and worthy of praise, it will be noticed. Humility promises honor and recognition. This was certainly the case with the godly woman in Proverbs 31. She didn't run around telling everyone what a great wife she was or how well she managed her finances and her household. She was so humble she even served her servants, rising while it was still dark to fix breakfast for them. Whatever she did, she did to the fullest, with loving commitment.

What did she receive in return? Her husband and her children praised her and everyone in the community knew the kind of woman she was. She was known because she feared the Lord and was accomplished at her work. Her humility brought her honor.

The prophet Micah summed it up this way. "What does the Lord require of you but to . . . walk humbly with your God?" (Mic. 6:8). Surely, our lives will be easier and freer from the encumberances of sin if we heed his advice and remember that, "When pride comes, then comes dishonor, but with the humble is wisdom" (Prov. 11:2).

Workshop

1. In this chapter we have seen that pride has many faces. This is reflected in the original Hebrew language, where many different words are used to express the various nuances about this sin.

Read the Hebrew definition, look up each verse then substitute the Hebrew meaning for the word "proud" or "pride." The first one is done for you.

a. GEAH: a state of being proud   Proverbs 8:13

"The fear of the Lord is to hate evil."
The state of being proud and arrogant.

b. GAAVAH: exaltation   Proverbs 14:3

c. GAOWN: rising, excellency   Proverbs 16:18

d. ZADON: presumptuous   Proverbs 21:24

e. GEEH: lofty, proud   Proverbs 16:19

f. RUWM: high, lofty   Proverbs 6:17

g. RACHAB: broad, wide, expansive   Proverbs 21:4

h. GABAHH: haughty   Proverbs 16:5

2. Some famous nonbiblical proverbs about pride and humility are listed. Read each one and write your own interpretation of it.

    a. Pride hides our faults to us and magnifies them to others (anon.).

    b. A person who talks about his inferiority hasn't one (Hawaiian).

c. Do you wish people to speak well of you? Don't yourself (Pascal).

d. The man who never alters his opinion is like standing water and breeds reptiles of the mind (William Blake).

e. A fool always finds a greater fool to admire him (Nicholas Boileau).

f. Pride that dines on vanity, sups on contempt (Benjamin Franklin).

g. The empty vessel makes the greatest sound (anon.).

h. The greatest fault is to be conscious of none (Thomas Lyle).

i. Many people are esteemed merely because they are not known (French).

j. It is a sign that your reputation is small if your own tongue must praise you (Sir Matthew Hale).

k. Conceit may puff a man up but never prop him up (John Ruskin).

3. The dictionary gives many definitions of the word pride. Look up each of the synonyms for "proud" and write it in the space next to the word.

    a. conceited

    b. vain

    c. boastful

    d. insolent

    e. patronizing

    f. supercilious

    g. disdainful

    h. inflated

    i. bloated

    j. smug

Now do the same with these synonyms for "humble."

    a. suppliant

    b. modest

    c. unassuming

    d. unpretentious

e. demure

f. gentle

g. meek

h. deferential

Notes

1. W. B. Eerdmans, Pulpit Commentary, *Proverbs*.
2. C. I. Scofield, *Scofield Correspondence Course* (Chicago: Moody Bible Institute, n.d.), vol. 2, p. 302.

NINE

Enemies and Friends

A friend loves at all times.
Proverbs 17:17

I was watching an old mystery movie on the late show the other night. A few moments into the film the inevitable body turned up. As the star detective interviewed the suspects, one of them said, "I can't imagine who would have wanted to kill Harry. He doesn't have an enemy in the world," to which the investigator replied, "Everyone has enemies."

I'm afraid that's true. Adults, children, men, women, Christians, atheists—all of us are plagued in some way by people who dislike or even hate us for one reason or another. Sometimes we "make" enemies. We alienate or offend people and they become our adversaries. Their dislike may or may not be justified. Nevertheless, they are enemies.

Sometimes people simply dislike us for no apparent reason. They may be threatened by us, differ with what we believe or have what is commonly referred to as a "personality clash." Unwilling to live and let live, they are antagonistic toward us; they choose to live at war with us, sometimes overtly attacking, other times waging a cold war of criticism or manipulation.

We acquire some of our enemies because we are on opposing sides when it comes to issues. Homosexuals view Anita Bryant as an enemy. Many Jews felt the same way about Christians who participated in Campus Crusade for Christ's "I've Found It" campaign. They retaliated with a "We Never Lost It" movement.

Frequently, in these kinds of rival situations, the antagonism is limited to the cause that's involved, and the people—apart from that area—may like each other. Many times we see politicians berate, belittle and downgrade each other, then shake hands and go play golf together.

So, there are different kinds of enemies who assail us in various ways; but no matter how they come packaged, they are hard to cope with. And because we don't know how to handle them or our feelings about them (we hate back and they make us angry!), we let them inflict needless pain and stress on us. As they interfere with our lives, we want to retaliate, thereby intensifying the problem.

How to Handle an Enemy

The book of Proverbs contains sound advice on how to handle an enemy, which indicates God knew we would have them. They are a part of life; an outgrowth of our basic sin nature. We cannot avoid them but we can eliminate the influence they exert over us.

First of all we are not to seek revenge. We have to be honest enough to admit we want to "get" our enemies; that we want revenge. We want to defend ourselves against further attack, hurt them back, get even, retaliate. The Lord knows this will be our reaction so He tells us we must not try to get back at our foes. "Do not say, 'Thus I shall do to him as he has done to me; I will render to the man according to his work' " (Prov. 24:29). He instructs us against that faulty course of action called revenge. "Do not say, 'I will repay evil'; wait for the Lord, and He will save you" (20:22). That little verse contains two commands and a promise. We are not to try to repay evil for evil. God, who is perfect justice, is equipped to handle the wrongs we suffer but we are not. Reprisal will only make things worse so we are told not to wage any counterattacks against our enemies.

Rather we are told to wait for the Lord. We don't like to do that. We want immediate justice, instant vindication; but God says wait and when we do He will save us. We cannot deliver ourselves from our enemies! We cannot save ourselves! We have to forget about our foes and concentrate on our relationship with the Lord. When we obey, when we do what He asks, we have victory and the Lord is free to defeat our enemies without any interference from us.

"When a man's ways are pleasing to the Lord, He makes even his enemies to be at peace with him" (16:7). We cannot make our enemies be at peace with us, but God can when we relinquish control of them to Him.

We must also control our emotions toward those who dislike us and whom we dislike. It is normal to hate someone who is making your life miserable; who does you an injustice, lies about you, hurts your feelings or misjudges you; who undermines you to others or manipulates to put you in a bad light—and enemies do all those things and more. But no matter what they do to us we must not hate them.

If we hate our enemies we are letting them make us sin because. "He who despises his neighbor sins" (14:21). And beyond that, hating only causes more trouble. "Hatred stirs up strife" (10:12). Hatred does not harm our enemies; it debilitates *us*.

In dealing with an adversary, we have to squelch our inclination to overract; *we need to control our actions as well* as our feelings. We are warned, "Do not go out hastily to argue your case; otherwise, what will you do in the end, when your [enemy] puts you to shame?" (25:8). If we wage a verbal battle against an enemy, when the time comes for us to present a legitimate argument, no one will listen and we will be embarrassed.

Instead of retaliating, hating or railing against our enemies, *we are supposed to minister to them;* to do whatever we can to aid and assist them. "If your enemy is hungry, give him food to eat; and if he is thirsty, give him water to drink; for you will heap burning coals on his head, and the Lord will reward you" (25:21,22). Difficult as it may be to put into practice, we should serve our enemies. We hurt ourselves if we fight with them; we will be blessed if we help them.

The Lord Jesus Christ presented this same idea when He taught, "Do not resist him who is evil; but whoever slaps you on your right cheek, turn to him the other also. . . . Love your enemies, and pray for those who persecute you" (Matt. 5:39,44). The message is clear: We are never relieved of our moral obligations because of the way someone treats us. There are no limits on God's love and there must be no restrictions on ours. That is why the Proverbs admonish us to maintain a loving, compassionate attitude toward our enemies, even when God deals with them on our behalf.

"*Do not rejoice when your enemy falls,* and do not let your heart be glad when he stumbles; lest the Lord see it and be displeased, and He turn away His anger from him" (Prov. 24:17,18). Hard, hard instruction. Hard not to cheer and clap your hands and dance around the room when your enemy falls. Hard not to laugh and be warm inside because he finally got what was coming to him.

But gloating when an enemy is defeated is a sin because we have been told not to. If we do rejoice, if we are internally pleased and smug, the Lord may back off when He is intervening for our benefit. Difficult as it may seem, all rules of

Christian conduct apply in our dealings with our enemies, and when we adhere to them they will make our lives easier.

Kinds of Friends

Just as there are different kinds of enemies, there are also various categories of friends.

Most of us have many acquaintances, people whom we know by name, whom we talk to on a superficial level and socialize with at times. One of the tellers at my bank is this kind of friend. We talk about our families, the weather, the cost of living. We have coffee together once in while. We enjoy each other but our relationship will never go beyond what it is now. Lillian is an acquaintance.

The mothers of the boys on Brian's Little League team are acquaintances, too. We have been drawn together by a mutual interest. We talk, joke and bemoan the bad calls the umpires make; then in June when the season ends we will go our separate ways.

Then there are people who are what I call friends. Our relationships with them are based on mutual goals and interests and the fact that we like them and have fun together. They are our "buddies," the people we enjoy doing things with. We usually have fewer friends than we do acquaintances. In this level of association, complaints are aired and confidences shared but there are limits to what we disclose. We usually rely on these friends for physical company rather than emotional support.

A third kind of friends are people who could be referred to as comrades, confidants or companions. They are the chosen few—for none of us have a lot of these kinds of close friends—who know us inside out. These friends go through our problems and our griefs, bear our burdens with us, are there for us to share our sorrows and joys, and uphold us when we need help. They love, understand and accept us, just as we are.

Dinah Murlock described this type of friend in this way. "Oh, the comfort—the inexpressible comfort of feeling safe with a person; having neither to weigh thoughts nor measure words, but pouring them all right out, just as they are, chaff and grain together, certain that a faithful hand will take and sift them, keep what is worth keeping and with a breath of kindness, blow the rest away."

The Proverbs refer to another kind of friend: our neighbor. A neighbor is anyone whose life touches ours or who lives next to or near us. Neighbors are people who, because of geographical location or circumstances, come into contact with us and become an incorporated part of our existence.

We all need friends at each of these levels. There is no doubt that friends make life more enjoyable and palatable. Without them we would be lonely and isolated, unable to know ourselves as we should.

God has recorded some important ground rules for friendship in the book of Proverbs. Learning and understanding these rules will not only make us better friends and improve the quality of our ongoing interpersonal relationships, but will help us make more friends, and perhaps reinstitute some damaged or stagnant friendships.

To Have and Be a Friend

Ralph Waldo Emerson said, "The only way to have a friend is to be one." But what does friendship involve? How can we be friends in the purest sense? Friendship is based in two things: love and loyalty. "A friend loves at all times" (Prov. 17:17). He loves when he disagrees with his friend. He remains faithful when his friend slights him or gets angry at him. He rejoices when good things happen to his friend and sorrows when he is in pain. Circumstances do not alter his attitudes or actions toward him. He unequivocally, unselfishly, loves at *all* times.

Loving at all times is synonymous with loyalty. Ultimately, "That which is desired in a man is loyalty" (19:22,

AMP). He remains steadfast in his commitment to a relationship, no matter what. He is faithful.

Love and loyalty are displayed in several ways. Since "love covers all transgressions" (10:12), and "he who covers a transgression seeks love" (17:9), a real friend is forgiving and understanding about the faults and failings of his associates. He is keenly aware of his own imperfections and knows that, "Two persons will not be friends long if they cannot forgive each other's failings."

He is always ready to support and lend a helping hand. He will not let a friend go through a trial alone; he is always there, willing to do whatever needs to be done. He "sticks closer than a brother" (18:24).

Such friends are hard to find. "Many a man proclaims his own loyalty, but who can find a trustworthy [friend]?" (20:6). If we are going to be, and therefore have, faithful friends we must covenant in our hearts to love and stick close to them at all times. As we do we will be blessed because, "A faithful man will abound with blessings" (28:20).

Friendship, like all other areas of our lives, is governed by certain standards. The Proverbs list many "thou shalts" and "thou shalt nots" about interpersonal relationships.

The first don't of friendship is don't be selfish. "Do not withhold good from those to whom it is due, when it is in your power to do it" (3:27). We have to be willing to share our time, emotions and perhaps our material substance with our friends. We are obligated to help them if we possibly can.

Second, don't build a friendship on superficial ground. We should not attach ourselves to someone because of what they have or the position they hold. Solomon noted that, "Many will entreat the favor of a generous man, and every man is a friend to him who gives gifts" (19:6). Friendship can't be bought. It must be based on mutual admiration and interests, on what we can give, not merely on what we can get out of it.

Third, do not take advantage of your friends or use the friendship to manipulate them into doing things that are against their better judgment. "The exceedingly grasping, covetous and violent man entices his neighbor, leading him into the way that is not good" (16:29, *AMP*). We should be aware that our friends may follow our example—go where we go, do what we do, want what we want—so we should try to exert a positive influence, not a self-serving one.

Fourth, don't pick fights. When we know someone well sometimes we take out our bad moods on them. We vent our anger on them and look for things to criticize. Proverbs 3:30 says, "Do not contend with a man without cause, if he has done you no harm." This implies there will be times when we have a legitimate reason to disagree with a friend and hassle things out with him, but we should not purposely agitate for no reason or do so without cause.

Even if we do have a valid reason for contending with a friend, we should do it in a pleasant, reasonable manner. If we are justifiably angry, we still should hold our tongue and keep our cool. "He who restrains his words has knowledge, and he who has a cool spirit is a man of understanding" (17:27).

Yelling, accusing, ranting and raving won't help, but, "a soft tongue breaks the bone" (25:15). Don't borrow trouble. "The beginning of strife is like letting out water, so abandon the quarrel before it breaks out" (17:14). Be a peacemaker. Rely on the fact that "the slow to anger pacifies contention" (15:18). Simply put, it is best not to pick quarrels with our friends.

Fifth, don't be stubborn. Remember, love does not demand its own way. We have to give and take in a friendship, compromise and sometimes do what someone else wants. "He who willfully separates and estranges himself [from God and man] seeks his own desire" (18:1, *AMP*). Willfulness can destroy a friendship.

A sixth don't is do not meddle. Just because someone is a friend does not give us carte blanche to interfere in his or her personal affairs. "Like one who takes a dog by the ears is he who passes by and meddles with strife not belonging to him" (26:17). We should not offer advice unless we are asked. We are to support our friends, not interfere with them. We shouldn't push for details if someone does not want to confide in us. We should go only as far as we are invited.

Seventh, don't overdo a relationship. When I was a little girl we called this "wearing out your welcome." There is such a thing as too much togetherness. The Proverbs advise, "Let your foot rarely be in your neighbor's house, lest he become weary of you and hate you" (25:17). Even the best of friends need breathing room, time away from one another. The quality of the time spent together is more important than quantity. We also have to allow for other relationships in our friends' lives. We will not be the only person they are close to.

The eighth and final don't in Proverbs is don't talk about your friends. In a previous chapter we saw in detail how gossip can corrode and damage relationships. Proverbs 17:9 says that repeating a matter, verbally breaking trust by revealing a confidence, "separates *intimate* friends." Instead, a wise woman "opens her mouth in wisdom, and the teaching of kindness is on her tongue" (31:26).

We can even overdo compliments. "He who blesses his friend with a loud voice early in the morning, it will be reckoned a curse to him" (27:14). We would do well and protect those precious relationships if we remember that even when we are saying nice things that, "When there are many words, transgression is unavoidable, but he who restrains his lips is wise" (10:19).

On the positive side, Proverbs offers me "do's" of friendship.

The first do is choose friends carefully, because they

exert a powerful influence on how we think and act. "He who walks with wise men will be wise, but the companion of fools will suffer harm" (13:20).

We are affected by the company we keep. An old Chinese proverb observes, "He who lies with dogs will get fleas." The Lord warns us, "Do not associate with a man given to anger; or go with a hot-tempered man, lest you learn his ways, and find a snare for yourself" (22:24,25). We are cautioned not to "be with heavy drinkers of wine, or with gluttonous eaters of meat; for the heavy drinker and the glutton will come to poverty" (23:20,21).

We are told to steer clear of people who pretend to be our friends but who have ulterior motives for wanting to associate with us. God does not want His righteous ones to be misused. We are instructed, "Do not eat the bread of a selfish man, or desire his delicacies; for as he thinks within himself, so he is. He says to you, 'Eat and drink!' but his heart is not with you. You will vomit up the morsel you have eaten, and waste your [pleasant words]" (23:6-8). Some people are not worthy of our friendship.

Our friends also affect what others think about us. Since "a good name is to be more desired than great riches" (22;1), we should not build relationships with people who might detract from our respectability. The apostle Paul commanded the Corinthians, "Do not be bound together with unbelievers; for what partnership have righteousness and lawlessness, or what fellowship has light with darkness?" (2 Cor. 6:14).

If this is to be our standard, what about the fact that Christ was criticized for being with wine-bibbers and gluttons? Or that He went to the house of a hated tax collector named Zaccheus? Or that prostitutes and thieves were named among His followers? Obviously, if we follow the Lord's example, these admonitions cannot mean we should separate ourselves from such people but that we must control the level of the relationship.

We should be *with* them but never enter into any deep, permanent, abiding relationship. We are not to walk with sinners, intermingle our life-style with theirs. We should not be bound to, associate regularly with, be companions of, or socialize on a regular basis with the ungodly—with those who walk in darkness.

Another proverbial rule of friendship is, be understanding. "It is [a friend's] glory to overlook a transgression" (Prov. 19:11). When someone we care about hurts our feelings or wrongs us, we must be willing to overlook it. That means we won't give a second thought to a slight or expect an apology but simply ignore it. In doing so we avoid making fools of ourselves, because "Keeping away from strife is an honor for a man, but any fool will quarrel" (20:3).

We strengthen a friendship when we downplay friction because by being understanding we acknowledge our own fallibility. After all, who are we to criticize or condemn our friends? "Who can say, 'I have cleansed my heart, I am pure from my sin'?" (20:9). If we want friends to deal kindly with us when we disappoint them, we must deal kindly with them.

Third, we should be available to our friends, to undergird their efforts and share both their joys and sorrows. "A friend . . . sticks closer than a brother" (18:24). Sharing is intrinsic to friendship. Our son Brian is adopted, and I will never forget the day we went to pick him up. When we got home dozens of our friends came over to see him and share that blessed time with us. They had waited with us for 11 months for his arrival and made the occasion even more special by being there for us to "show off" our new addition.

Nor will I forget when George was rushed to the hospital after a mild heart attack, for open heart surgery. His brother and mother came, and of course our daughters were there with me, and our pastor. But, I felt the family was relying on my strength and I wasn't sure I could maintain my sanity for the six to eight hours the surgery takes.

I still do not have words to explain the relief and happiness I felt when, after they hauled my husband off to the operating room, I walked into the lobby to begin the long vigil and my friend, Emarie, was there. She took me down to the cafeteria for coffee. She knew I would need to get off by myself for part of the time with someone I could talk to about my fears. We talked about old friends and good times we'd had together. She prayed with me and stayed until we were told that the operation was a success and that George would be fine.

I could not have made it without her, and I will always love her in a special way for being there with me without being asked—for sticking by me when I desperately needed a friend.

A fourth "do" of friendship is that we should encourage our friends. We should be builders in their lives. We should cheer them with our presence and our words. "Anxiety in the heart of a man weighs it down, but a good word makes it glad" (12:25). We should share our joys with them and try to be bearers of glad tidings because, "Good news puts fat on the bones" (15:30).

We should encourage our friends by saying what they need to hear, what will uplift not discourage them. Someone once said, "If your friend is a help, a joy, and inspiration to you, tell him. There are discouraged hearts everywhere just hungry for appreciation and sympathy."

Just the other day I was worried about something and when I shared my concern with my friend, Lorrie, she said exactly what I needed to hear. She said, "Well, if it does happen, I know you can handle it and I'll be there to help. But if it doesn't, you're wasting your time worrying for nothing." In a loving, kind way she pointed out that I was being foolish, and at the same time she promised her support if I needed it.

We also build up our friends by being ourselves, not by trying to conform to what we think they want us to be or saying what they want us to say. I know things and have had experiences that my friends have not. My friends know things and have lived through circumstances I have not faced. Therefore, we can contribute to each other's maturity and understanding.

Solomon noted that as "iron sharpens iron, so one man sharpens another" (27:17). God uses friends as a gentle abrasive to sandpaper the rough edges of our personalities; to teach and mellow us and conform us more closely to the image of Christ.

I have learned many things about being a good mother from my dear friend, another Jo. She has faced many heart-breaking situations with her three children but through them all she abided in God's love and stuck by her kids through thick and thin. She never lost hope or doubted God. She taught me a great deal about what faith and staying power can accomplish. She "sharpened" me as a mother.

We should also encourage our friends with our counsel. "A man's counsel [should be] sweet to his friend" (27:9). When we offer opinions or advice we must be sure we are not just imposing our beliefs but suggesting what is best for our friends that will uplift and hearten them. When we counsel, we need to be empathetic—put ourselves in their shoes—and offer ideas that will help, not hinder; soothe, not agitate; comfort, not disturb. We can encourage with "sweet" counsel.

A fifth basic of friendship is do be open and honest. We should care enough about our friends to confront them when they are straying from the path of righteousness. Proverbs 27:5,6 asserts that, "Better is open rebuke than love that is concealed. Faithful are the wounds of a friend."

Love means we accept our friends' imperfections but it does not mean we tolerate their sin because love "does not rejoice in unrighteousness, but rejoices with the truth" (1 Cor. 13:6). A real friend cares enough about the people he is close to, to tell them the truth about themselves when it needs to be said. Sometimes a loving friend is forced to openly rebuke an associate.

Truthful confrontation, directness and honest criticism may hurt. There will be times when we are injured by a "faithful wound" from a friend, or when we hurt a beloved companion by being forthright with her or him, but God will use our concerns to help and heal because, "The righteous is a guide to his [friend]" (Prov. 12:26).

The issue isn't whether we should confront but how we do it. When Christ confronted the woman at the well He did not rail at her for being divorced five times and living with a man who was not her husband. He calmly and gently verbalized her sin to her. "He said to her. 'Go call your husband, and come here.' The woman answered and said, 'I have no husband.' Jesus said to her, 'You have well said, "I have no husband"; for you have had five husbands; and the one whom you now have is not your husband; this you have said truly' " (John 4:16-18).

And when He dealt with the woman caught in adultery, He treated her with respect. He helped her save face and maintain her dignity. He called her "woman" not prostitute, harlot or tramp. He did not accuse or condemn her. He let her know that what she was doing was unworthy of her and that He expected better of her. "Jesus said, 'Neither do I condemn you; go your way; from now on sin no more' " (John 8:11). He showed her that He trusted her, that He knew she could improve and become a better person.

When we rebuke a friend, we have to do as Christ did: point out his sin then trust him to do what is right. We must not put restrictions on him, lay down ultimatums or condemn him, but be there to help restore him.

What kind of friend are you? Are you loyal? Jesus said, "Greater love has no one than this, that one lay down his life

for his friends" (John 15:13). Are you loving? "God so loved the world, that He gave His only begotten Son" (John 3:16). The Lord is our supreme example of what a friend should be. If we follow His example and adhere to His standards we will become "a friend [who] loves at all times" (Prov. 17:17), and our lives and relationships will be richer for it.

Workshop

1. Look up each of the proverbs then summarize, in your own words, how it could apply to being a loving, loyal friend.

Reference	Action
3:3	
3:29	
6:1-3	
9:7-9	
11:12	
11:14	
18:19	
21:13	
22:9	
25:13	
26:18,19	

2. Some famous nonbiblical proverbs about friends and enemies are listed here. Read each one and write your interpretation of it.

   a. 'Tis thus that on the choice of friends our good or evil name depends (John Gay).

   b. Show me your enemies and I'll tell you your stature (anon.).

   c. He that hath no friend hath weak legs (Persian).

   d. Tell me the company you keep and I'll tell you who you are (anon.).

   e. A true friend is someone who holds you to your best self (Amos R. Wells).

   f. Reprove a friend privately, commend him publicly (anon.).

   g. He who has a thousand friends has not one friend to spare,
      He who has one enemy will meet him everywhere (Arabic).

   h. Birds of a feather will fly together (anon.).

i. Friendship is the only thing in the world concerning the usefulness of which all mankind are agreed (Cicero).

j. Familiarity breeds contempt (anon.).

k. A friendship is to be valued for what there is in it, not for what can be gotten out of it (H. Clay Trumbull).

l. A broken friendship may be soldered but it will never be sound (anon.).

Note

1. C. I. Scofield, *Scofield Correspondence Course,* Old Testament (Chicago: Moody Bible Institute, n.d.), vol. 2, p. 302.